US and Azerbaijani Oil in the Nineteenth Century

The Two Titans

US and Azerbaijani Oil in the Nineteenth Century

The Two Titans

Marius S. Vassiliou and Mir-Yusif Mir-Babayev

LEXINGTON BOOKS
Lanham • Boulder • New York • London

Published by Lexington Books
An imprint of The Rowman & Littlefield Publishing Group, Inc.
4501 Forbes Boulevard, Suite 200, Lanham, Maryland 20706
www.rowman.com

86–90 Paul Street, London EC2A 4NE

British Library Cataloguing in Publication Information Available

Library of Congress Cataloging-in-Publication Data
Names: Vassiliou, M. S., author. | Mir-Babaev, M. F. (Mir-I͡Usif Fazilogly), author.
Title: US and Azerbaijani oil in the nineteenth century : the two titans / Marius S. Vassiliou and Mir-Yusif Mir-Babayev.
Description: Lanham : Lexington Books, [2022] | Includes bibliographical references and index.
Identifiers: LCCN 2022034570 (print) | LCCN 2022034571 (ebook) | ISBN 9781793629524 (cloth) | ISBN 9781793629531 (ebook)
Subjects: LCSH: Petroleum industry and trade—United States—History—19th century. | Petroleum industry and trade—Azerbaijan—History—19th century.
Classification: LCC HD9565 .V44 2022 (print) | LCC HD9565 (ebook) | DDC 338.2/72820973—dc23/eng/20220826
LC record available at https://lccn.loc.gov/2022034570
LC ebook record available at https://lccn.loc.gov/2022034571

US and Azerbaijani Oil in the Nineteenth Century

The Two Titans

Marius S. Vassiliou and Mir-Yusif Mir-Babayev

LEXINGTON BOOKS
Lanham • Boulder • New York • London

Published by Lexington Books
An imprint of The Rowman & Littlefield Publishing Group, Inc.
4501 Forbes Boulevard, Suite 200, Lanham, Maryland 20706
www.rowman.com

86–90 Paul Street, London EC2A 4NE

British Library Cataloguing in Publication Information Available

Library of Congress Cataloging-in-Publication Data
Names: Vassiliou, M. S., author. | Mir-Babaev, M. F. (Mir-I͡Usif Fazilogly), author.
Title: US and Azerbaijani oil in the nineteenth century : the two titans / Marius S. Vassiliou and Mir-Yusif Mir-Babayev.
Description: Lanham : Lexington Books, [2022] | Includes bibliographical references and index.
Identifiers: LCCN 2022034570 (print) | LCCN 2022034571 (ebook) | ISBN 9781793629524 (cloth) | ISBN 9781793629531 (ebook)
Subjects: LCSH: Petroleum industry and trade—United States—History—19th century. | Petroleum industry and trade—Azerbaijan—History—19th century.
Classification: LCC HD9565 .V44 2022 (print) | LCC HD9565 (ebook) | DDC 338.2/72820973—dc23/eng/20220826
LC record available at https://lccn.loc.gov/2022034570
LC ebook record available at https://lccn.loc.gov/2022034571

Contents

Acknowledgments

We thank Ray Sorenson for useful discussions during the early stages of this book. We also owe a debt of gratitude to the library of George Mason University, Fairfax, Virginia.

Introduction

This book is a brief history of oil in the nineteenth century, in the United States and the Russian Empire. These two entities were responsible for about 97 percent of the world's oil production over the century, and over the course of the century, nearly all the Russian Empire's oil production came from the territory that is now the independent state of Azerbaijan. Hence, the book is about the history of oil in the United States and Azerbaijan from 1800 to 1900. In most Western literature, the United States is covered far more exhaustively than Azerbaijan; we seek to rectify that imbalance.

In the United States, the modern phase of the oil industry began in 1859 with the drilling of the Drake well in Pennsylvania, but there was an oil trade predating that well. In Azerbaijan, the truly modern industry began in 1872 with Tsar Alexander II's promulgation of rules promoting competitive private-sector business. However, a documented oil trade has existed there since ancient times, and in 1846, a quarter century before the tsar's liberalization, the first industrial oil well in the world was drilled near Baku, Azerbaijan, under imperial government auspices.

The oil industry before the twentieth century was focused on producing kerosene that could be burned in lamps for illumination. Other uses of products obtainable from crude oil included lubrication and perceived medicinal benefits. Some crude oil and heavy refined products were also burned for energy, but the dramatic transition from illumination to energy did not occur until after the turn of the twentieth century.

LIMITATIONS

In our exposition, we follow some limiting principles:

- This book is about oil, not gas. We occasionally discuss natural gas in some contexts but make no effort to cover gas in the same depth as oil.
- The book is mostly restricted to the nineteenth century. We do discuss earlier eras as background, and we also briefly mention a few important events that happened soon after the turn of the twentieth century, such as the discovery of Spindletop and the breakup of Standard Oil, but the bulk of our effort is devoted to the nineteenth century.
- We rarely stray away from the United States and Azerbaijan. We do not cover important developments in Romania, Canada, and Austro-Hungarian Galicia, for example, except briefly in chapter 4 when considering candidates for "the world's first modern oil well."
- We make no pretensions at an exhaustive history; our treatment is selective and seeks to elucidate major themes.

PLAN OF THE BOOK

In the first chapter, we characterize oil production in the nineteenth century by presenting and discussing various statistics to clarify which countries, regions, and oil fields were the important producers. In the second, we discuss the nineteenth century's main application for oil products: illumination. We compare kerosene to other illuminants, discuss kerosene production in the United States and Azerbaijan, and briefly consider the question of whether the petroleum industry saved the world's whales from extinction (it didn't—but it probably helped). In chapter 3, we survey the history of oil in the United States and Azerbaijan before the start of the nineteenth century—a history that is particularly rich in the case of Azerbaijan. We then move on to consider the question, in chapter 4, of who drilled the first modern oil well. According to some relevant criteria, the first modern well was drilled in Azerbaijan in 1846; according to other criteria, it was the 1859 Drake well in Pennsylvania. In chapter 5, we present a history of nineteenth-century oil in the United States without repeating those specific portions of history discussed in chapter 4. In chapter 6, we do likewise for Azerbaijan. Chapters 5 and 6 concentrate on events, regions, and businesses. Chapter 7 discusses the development of oil-related science and technology in the nineteenth century, including exploration, drilling, refining, and transport. Both the United States and Azerbaijan made important contributions to technology. Finally, in chapter 8 we make some brief concluding remarks. The appendices present some important production statistics in tabular form, some not readily available until now outside Russia or Azerbaijan. The appendices also contain brief biographical data on important people involved in the petroleum business and technology as well as a chronology.

RUSSIA OR AZERBAIJAN?

In this book we refer repeatedly to the nineteenth-century "Azerbaijani" oil industry, but it is important to note that from 1828 onward, Azerbaijan was part of the Russian Empire. In the early part of the nineteenth century, Russia expanded into the southern Caucasus, at the expense of Iran. The area of Baku had actually been occupied by Russia before, as a result of the Russo-Persian War of 1722–1723, but it had reverted to Iranian rule soon after. However, in 1804 Russia invaded Iran and sacked the city of Ganja. Russia won the resulting Russo-Persian War of 1804–1813, and in 1813 gained Caucasian territory, including the Nakhichivan portion of today's Azerbaijan, in the Treaty of Gulistan. Russia violated the treaty, sparking another Russo-Persian War, lasting from 1826 to 1828, from which Russia emerged victorious. The 1828 Treaty of Turkmanchai saw Russia gain the rest of Azerbaijan, including the petroliferous Absheron peninsula (Hambly 2007, 162).

AZERBAIJAN, ABSHERON, OR BAKU?

We often refer to Azerbaijani oil interchangeably as "Azerbaijani oil," "Absheron oil," or "Baku oil." This is for the simple reason that the nineteenth century's major Azerbaijani oil fields were on the Absheron peninsula, ringing the Azerbaijani capital of Baku. This can be seen clearly on the sketch map in figure 6.1.

WESTERN VIRGINIA OR WEST VIRGINIA?

As we discuss in chapter 5, the state of West Virginia was formed during the American Civil War, as a large group of northwestern counties seceded from the then Confederate State of Virginia—a complex process in which oil interests played a nonnegligible role. West Virginia was formally admitted to the Union on June 20, 1863, as the thirty-fifth state. When discussing the oil industry prior to this date, we refer to the region as western Virginia. After that date, we refer to West Virginia.

Chapter 1

Characterizing Nineteenth-Century Oil Production

In this chapter, we characterize oil production in the nineteenth century by presenting and discussing various statistics to clarify which countries, regions, and oil fields were the important producers.

NINETEENTH-CENTURY WORLD OIL PRODUCTION WAS MINUSCULE BY MODERN STANDARDS

Nineteenth-century oil production began in earnest after Pennsylvania's Drake well in 1859, which is not to say that production was nonexistent before then, as we discuss in chapters 3–6. One important thing to understand about nineteenth-century oil production is that, by modern standards, it was minuscule. Total production of oil in the entire century was about 1.74 billion barrels. In contrast, the world in 2019 produced nearly that much (1.45 billion barrels) in just two weeks!

NINETEENTH-CENTURY WORLD OIL PRODUCTION WAS DOMINATED BY THE UNITED STATES AND AZERBAIJAN

Romania was the first country to begin officially recording oil production in 1857. The United States, Canada, and Russia followed, in 1861, 1862, and 1863, respectively. Figure 1.1 graphs oil production from 1859 to 1900; the dominance of the United States and Azerbaijan is immediately apparent. The United States was the largest producer in most years. Azerbaijan production exceeded US production in the years from 1898 to 1900. By 1902 the United

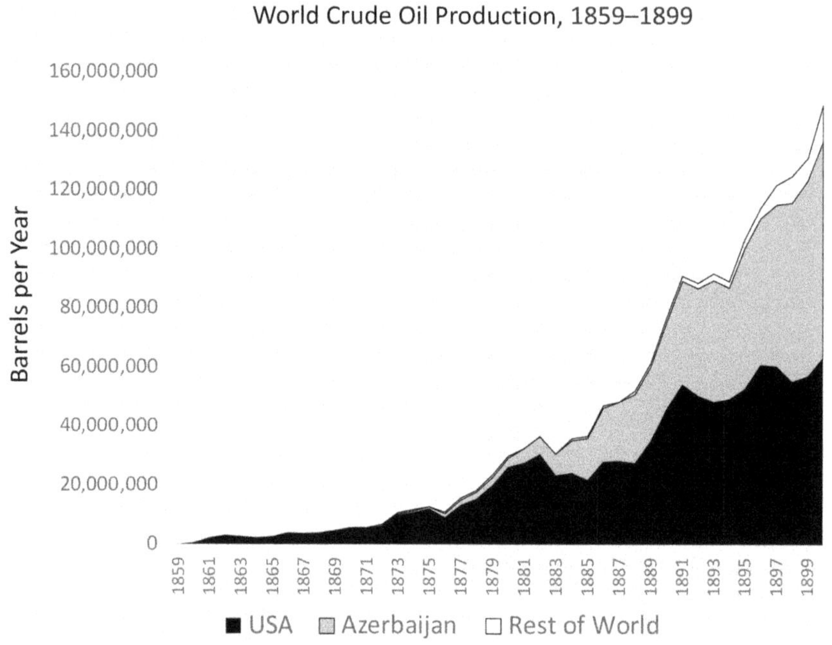

Figure 1.1. World Oil Production from 1859 to 1900, in Barrels per Year. The United States was the largest producer in most years. *Source*: Data from Oliphant (1901), Stowell (1885), and Day (1922).

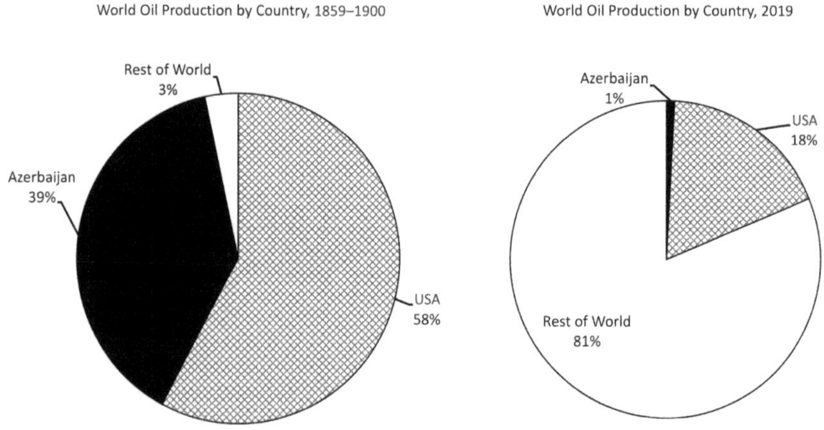

Figure 1.2. Contribution of the United States and Azerbaijan to World Oil Production during the Nineteenth Century and in 2019. *Source*: Data from Oliphant (1901), Stowell (1885), Day (1922), and BP (2020).

States would regain the lead. The United States accounted for 58 percent of all the oil produced from 1859 to 1900. Azerbaijan accounted for 39 percent, and the rest of the world 3 percent. Today the picture is very different: the United States accounted for 18 percent of all the oil produced in 2019, Azerbaijan just 1 percent, and the rest of the world 81 percent (figure 1.2).

NINETEENTH-CENTURY US PRODUCTION WAS DOMINATED BY PENNSYLVANIA AND NEIGHBORING STATES

For a significant part of the nineteenth century, the story of world oil production was largely a story of production in Azerbaijan and Pennsylvania. Analyzing production from 1859 to 1900 by region, we find (figure 1.3) that just three US states—Pennsylvania, West Virginia, and Ohio—accounted for over half of total world production. Pennsylvania alone accounted for 35 percent of world production, nearly the share of Azerbaijan.

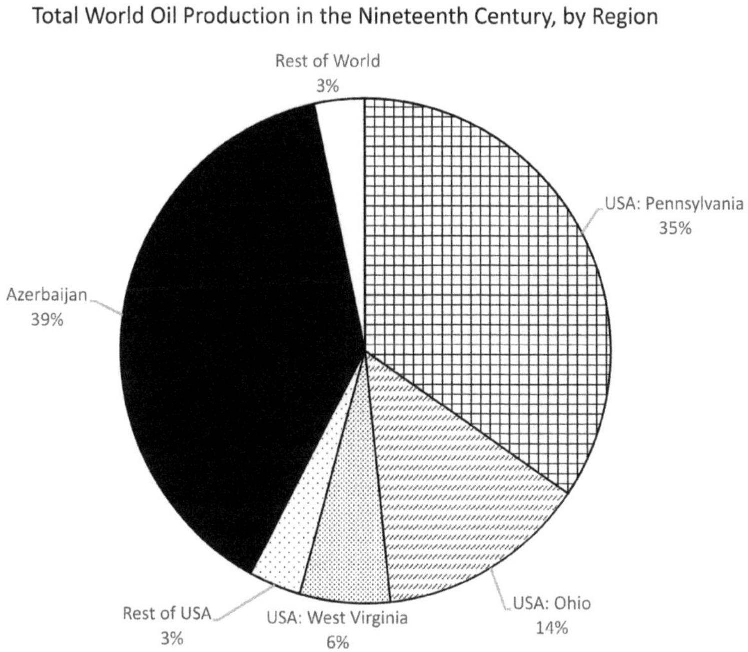

Figure 1.3. Total Production of Crude Oil in the World from 1859 to 1900 (1.74 Billion Barrels). In this chart, Pennsylvania includes New York production. *Source*: From data in Oliphant (1901), Stowell (1885), and Day (1922).

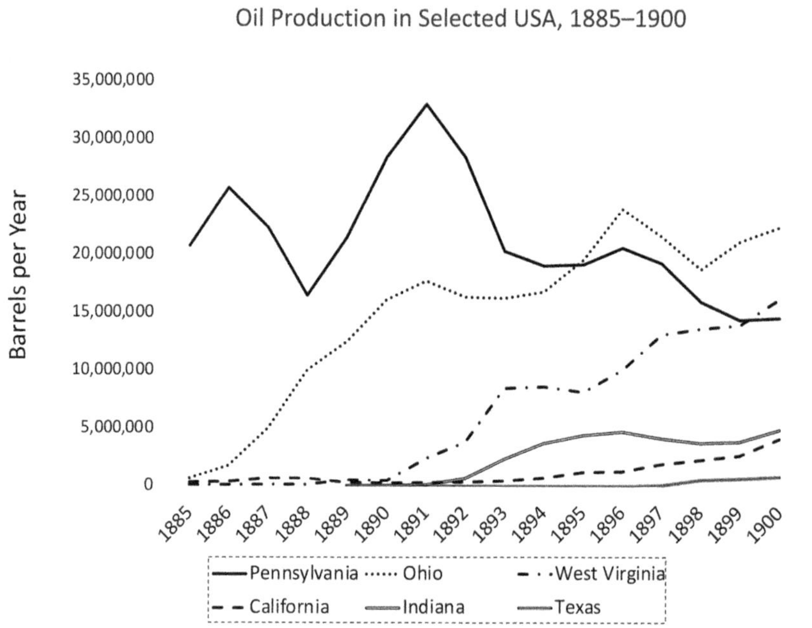

Figure 1.4. Oil Production in Selected US states, 1885–1900. Pennsylvania includes New York production. *Source*: From data in Day (1922).

Pennsylvania was thoroughly dominant in the United States before 1885. However, as shown in figure 1.4, Ohio surpassed it in 1895 and West Virginia in 1899. California, which would be exceedingly important in the twentieth century, began to become significant around the mid-1890s. Meanwhile, Texas, which would be even more important than California in the future, was only just beginning to make its presence felt toward the end of the 1800s. The map in figure 5.1 (chapter 5) depicts the established and emergent US production regions during the nineteenth century.

THE NINETEENTH-CENTURY TITANS DID NOT DOMINATE FOREVER

As we saw earlier, Azerbaijani and US oil production are much less important today than they were in the nineteenth century. It is also true that as new provinces were developed in the twentieth century, Azerbaijani

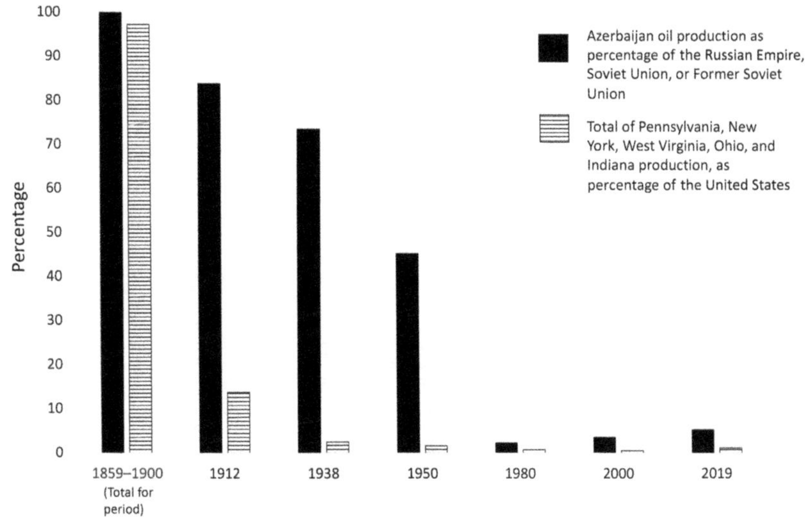

Figure 1.5. Decreasing dominance of Azerbaijan and Pennsylvania. Black bars show Azerbaijani oil production as a percent of total production in the Russian Empire, Soviet Union, or former Soviet Union. Patterned bars show production in Pennsylvania, New York, West Virginia, Ohio, and Indiana as a percentage of total production in the United States. *Source*: Calculated from data in Oliphant (1901), Stowell (1885), Day (1922), DeGolyer and MacNaughton (2018, 2020), Balayev (1969), BP (2020), and EIA (2012, 2020).

dominance eventually declined within Russia and the Soviet Union, as did the prominence of Pennsylvania and neighboring states within the United States. From 1859 to 1900, Azerbaijan accounted for essentially all oil production in the Russian Empire (figure 1.5). By 1912 this proportion declined to about 84 percent. The decline continued, until by 1980 Azerbaijan accounted for only 2.3 percent of the oil production in the Soviet Union, the successor state to the Russian Empire. Azerbaijan's proportion recovered somewhat thereafter: in 2019 it accounted for 5.3 percent of the oil produced by the countries formerly in the Soviet Union. The decline of Pennsylvania and other dominant nineteenth-century states as a percentage of US production was more precipitous. Pennsylvania, Ohio, West Virginia, and Indiana accounted for 97.2 percent of total US oil production from 1859 to 1900. By 1912 their percentage was already down to 13.8 percent, and in 2000 it was just 0.6 percent. It recovered somewhat to 1.2 percent in 2019, as hydraulic fracturing and horizontal drilling techniques boosted production.

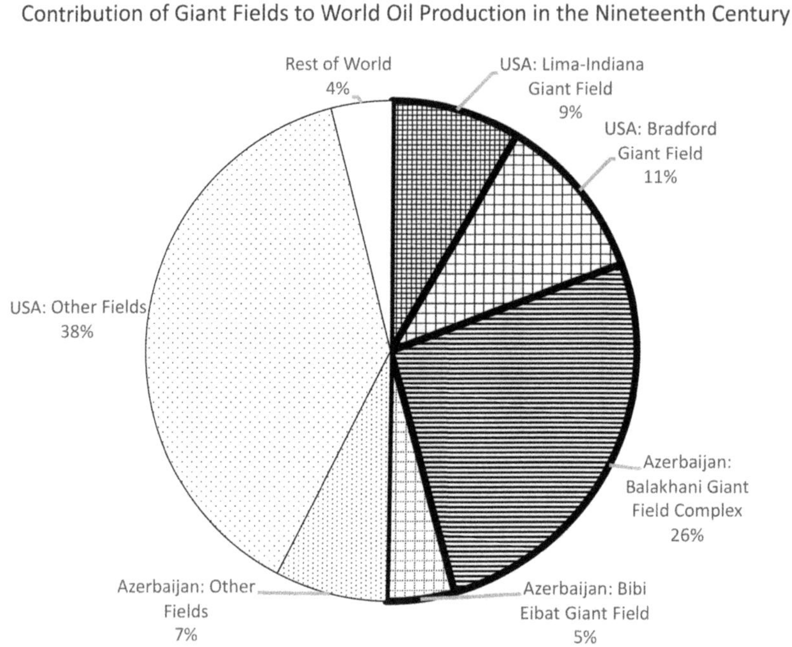

Figure 1.6. Total Production of Crude Oil in the World from 1859 to 1900 (1.74 Billion Barrels), Showing the Contribution of Giant Oil Fields. Giant oil fields are fields with ultimately recoverable oil of 500 million barrels or more. *Source*: From data in Oliphant (1898, 1901), Day (1922), and Fettke (1938, 292).

A FEW GIANT FIELDS DOMINATED NINETEENTH-CENTURY OIL PRODUCTION

During the nineteenth century, a large proportion of production came from a few giant oil fields. While there is some disagreement about what constitutes a giant oil field, a commonly accepted definition is that adopted by the American Association of Petroleum Geologists: a field with half a billion (500,000,000) barrels or more of estimated ultimately recoverable oil (Carmalt and Moscariello 2017, 10). Giant fields are extremely important for the world's oil supply. Only about 1 percent of the world's oil fields are giants, yet they account for approximately two-thirds to over three-fourths of the world's estimated recoverable oil resource. The hundred largest oil fields accounted for about 45 percent of the world's oil production in the mid-2000s.

During the nineteenth century, eleven giant fields were discovered. They are listed in table 1.1. Of the eleven giants, six were in the United States,

Table 1.1. Giant Oilfields Discovered in the Nineteenth Century

Name	*Country*	*Discovery year*	*Reservoir*	*Trap*	*Total oil in billion barrels*	*Size rank in 2021 among giant fields*
La Brea	Peru	1868	Sandstone	Fault block	1	249
Surakhani	Russian Empire: Azerbaijan	1870	Sandstone	Faulted anticline	0.9	281
Bradford	USA: Pennsylvania	1871	Sandstone	Anticline	0.658	391
Bibi-Eibat	Russian Empire: Azerbaijan	1871	Sandstone	Faulted anticline	2	119
Lima-Indiana	USA: Ohio-Indiana	1876	Carbonate	Anticline	0.514	487
Brea	USA: California	1884	Sandstone	Faulted anticline	0.439	593
Coalinga	USA: California	1887	Sandstone	Anticline	0.906	268
Starogroznyy	Russian Empire: Russia	1893	Sandstone	Other structural	0.65	397
Midway-Sunset	USA: California	1894	Sandstone	Anticline	2.692	95
Balakhani/ Sabunchi/ Romani	Russian Empire: Azerbaijan	1896	Sandstone	Anticline	2.4	102
Kern River	USA: California	1899	Sandstone	Anticline	1.676	147

Source: Horn (2021).

A giant oilfield is defined as one with at least half a billion barrels of ultimately recoverable oil.

four were in Azerbaijan, and one was in Peru. Of the US giants, only two were significantly developed before 1900—the Bradford field in Pennsylvania and New York and the Lima-Indiana field in Indiana and Ohio. In Azerbaijan, major production before 1900 only occurred in the Balakhani complex (Balakhani-Sabunchi-Romani) and in Bibi-Eibat. Balakhani alone accounted for 26 percent of all the production in the world over the course of the nineteenth century, while Bibi-Eibat accounted for another 5 percent. The two producing US giants, Lima-Indiana and Bradford, accounted for 20 percent of world production in the nineteenth century (see figure 1.6). Table D.5 gives detailed production histories for Lima-Indiana and Bradford, while table D.4 does so for Balakhani-Sabunchi-Romani and Bibi-Eibat. Surakhani did not see major production until the twentieth century. All the nineteenth-century giants were sandstone reservoirs, except for Lima-Indiana, which was carbonate. All were structural traps, and almost all anticlinal.

Chapter 2

Illumination

Nineteenth-Century Oil's "Killer App"

Oil has been used since ancient times for perceived medicinal purposes, lubrication, and illumination. All these uses continued into the nineteenth century, but it was illumination that truly drove the century's industrial-scale production, refinement, and marketing of oil. Even though heavy refined fractions of oil were burned for energy, particularly in Russia, the critical and central use of oil as an energy source was a feature of the twentieth century and beyond. In the 1860s when the boom in oil production began, the internal combustion engine was still decades in the future, as were industrial petrochemicals. The most important refined petroleum product in the nineteenth century was kerosene, intended to be burned in lamps for illumination.

ABRAHAM GESNER'S KEROSENE, 1846–1861

Although kerosene, as we have just noted, was an important product from refining petroleum, it was first obtained not from oil, but from coal. A Canadian geologist, Abraham Gesner, developed a distillation process in 1846 yielding an illuminating oil from bituminous coal. He developed the process further to take asphalt or bituminous shale as a feedstock and obtained a US patent in 1854. Gesner coined the term "kerosene," from the Greek words *keros* and *elaion* ("wax" and "oil").

Gesner intended to go into business producing kerosene from albertite, a type of asphalt found in Albert County, New Brunswick. He tried to obtain mining rights to an albertite-bearing property and came into conflict with other parties that had already filed claims on the same property to mine coal. Gesner claimed that albertite was not coal, but a mineral; he was able to convince a court in Halifax, Nova Scotia, of this fact. Unfortunately, the Nova

Scotia court's judgment was not honored in New Brunswick, and a New Brunswick court ruled against him, sidestepping the core issue of the nature of albertite by deciding that the coal mining leases covered minerals as well (Brice 2002).

Gesner left Canada and moved to New York in 1853. He obtained US patents for his processes and on June 27, 1854, assigned them to the new Asphalt Mining and Kerosene Gas Company, renamed as the North American Gas Light Company in 1856, and then as the New York Kerosene Oil Company in 1859. The feedstock was not albertite, but coal mined in Nova Scotia. It is possible that the refineries occasionally extracted kerosene from crude oil found in surface seeps in Pennsylvania before Edwin Drake drilled his well in 1859. If so, this was a portent of things to come, as petroleum would soon become the major source of kerosene. Gesner published a book (1861) on his distillation methods. In 1863 he sold his patents and returned to Canada, to become a professor at Dalhousie University in Nova Scotia. (For more information, see Beaton 1955; Brice 2002; Gray 2008b).

Other important early achievements in producing kerosene from crude oil are discussed in chapters 4–7. They include those of Ignacy Łukasiewicz in Austro-Hungarian Galicia; the Mehedinţeanu brothers in Romania; James Miller Williams in Ontario, Canada; Nikolai Voskoboinikov in Azerbaijan; and Samuel Kier and Andrés Pico in the United States.

THE AGE OF ILLUMINATION LASTED UNTIL THE TWENTIETH CENTURY

Harold Williamson and Arnold Daum produced a magisterial two-volume history (1959, 1963) of the American petroleum industry. They titled the first volume, covering the period from 1859 to 1899, the "Age of Illumination" and the second volume, covering 1899–1959, the "Age of Energy." Figure 2.1 shows how apt these titles were. It depicts the rapid transition from an illumination-dominated oil industry to an energy-dominated one in the United States. As late as 1899, petroleum products were used primarily for illumination. By 1919, they were primarily used for energy. During the nineteenth century, kerosene was used for illumination, while fuel oil and residual were used for energy, and gasoline was almost a waste product. By 1919 gasoline was a crucial energy product for motorized transport, and even about a third of the kerosene produced was used for energy rather than illumination (Williamson and Daum 1963).

In the period from 1883 to 1885, kerosene accounted for 82 percent of US refined petroleum products by volume. In Azerbaijan the percentage was lower, at 41.5 percent. Out of all Azerbaijani petroleum products,

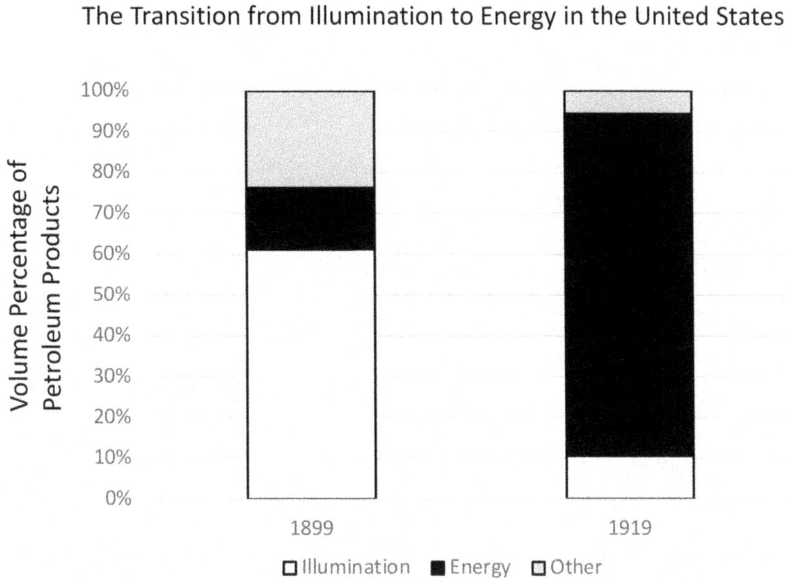

Figure 2.1. The Transition from Illumination to Energy in the United States: Volume Percentage of Refined Petroleum Products According to Use. As late as 1899, petroleum products were used primarily for illumination. By 1919 they were primarily used for energy. *Source*: Calculated from data in Williamson and Daum (1963, 168).

55.1 percent were residual heavy products, burned as fuel. This is depicted in figure 2.2. Part of the reason for this difference was the difference in composition between Azerbaijani and Pennsylvania oil, the former being richer in the heavier fractions.

Figure 2.3 shows the dramatic increase in the US production of kerosene, the refined product most relevant for illumination, between 1862 and 1885. Kerosene was also the primary petroleum product exported by the United States to the rest of the world, as shown in figure 2.4. Both volumetrically and in dollar terms, kerosene exports dwarfed those of crude oil, and other products such as naphtha. Europe remained the primary destination for US kerosene exports throughout the century, as shown in figure 2.5. However, Asia was also important, and it is interesting to note the dip in exports to Asia in the 1890s, as exports from Azerbaijan to that theater increased.

Azerbaijani production of kerosene for illumination was negligible until the 1870s, during which decade it grew rapidly. The 1880 production level in Azerbaijan was approximately fifty-six times that of 1872. Despite the rapid growth, Azerbaijan never quite caught up to the United States in production of illuminating oil, although it closed the gap considerably.

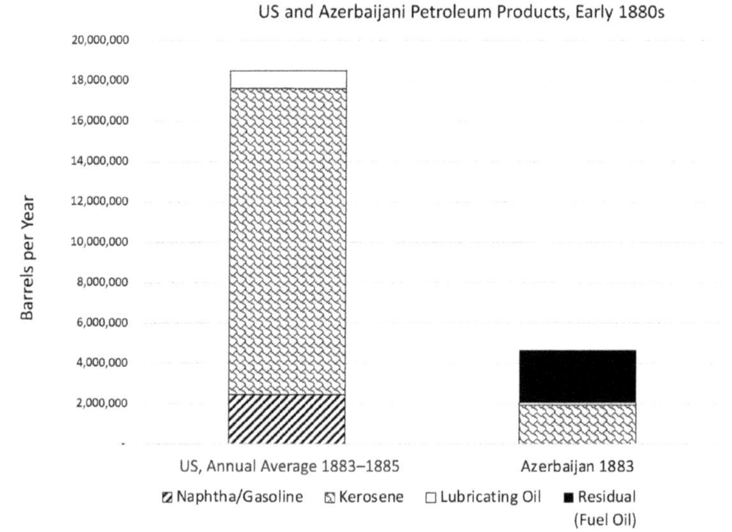

Figure 2.2. Comparison of US and Azerbaijani Output of Petroleum Products in the Early 1880s. US data are an annual average for 1883–1885. Azerbaijani data are for 1883. The United States had a considerably higher output overall, and kerosene constituted a higher proportion of its total. Also noteworthy is the importance of the heavy residual fraction in Azerbaijan's output. *Source*: Based on estimates in Williamson and Daum (1959, 485) and data in Baku Branch (1886, 128). Azerbaijani figures are converted from poods to barrels using values of 7.77 and 7.18 poods per barrel, respectively, for kerosene and gasoline. For lubricants and residual, a value of 9.22 poods per barrel is used.

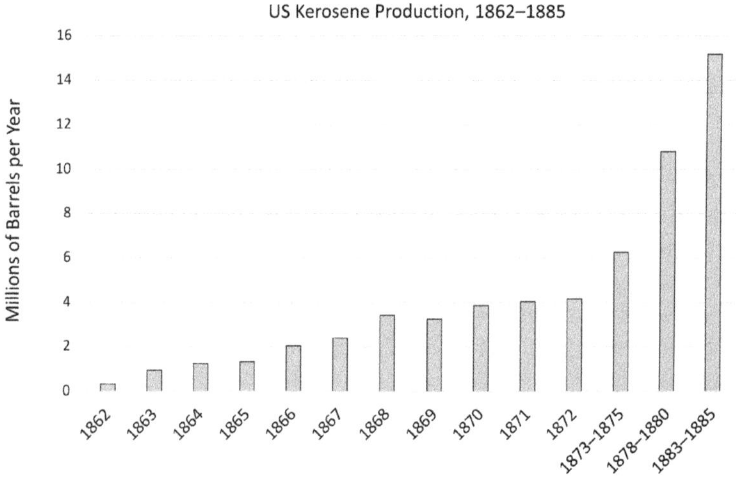

Figure 2.3. US Production of Kerosene, 1862–1885, in Millions of Barrels Per Year. Numbers for 1873–1875, 1878–1880, and 1883–1885 are annual averages for the respective time periods. *Source*: Based on data and estimates in Williamson and Daum (1959, 290, 485).

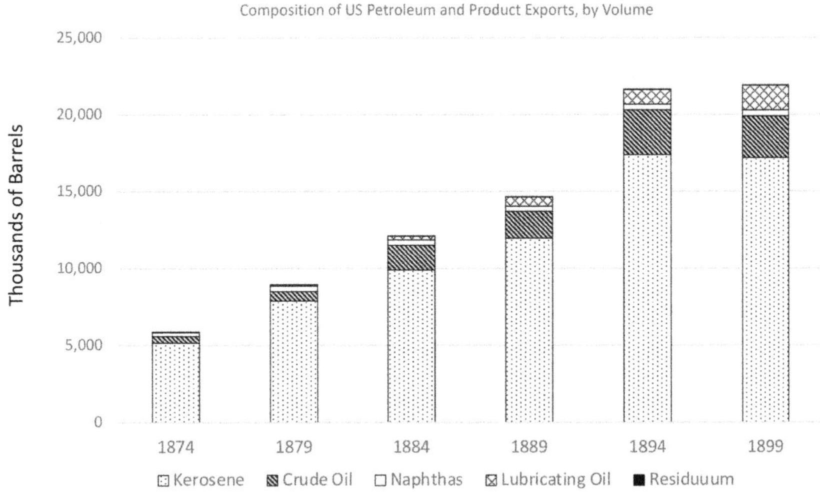

Figure 2.4. US Exports of Petroleum and Petroleum products, in Thousands of Barrels, for Years at Five-Year Intervals, Showing the Dominance of Kerosene. *Source*: From data tabulated in Williamson and Daum (1959, 742–757).

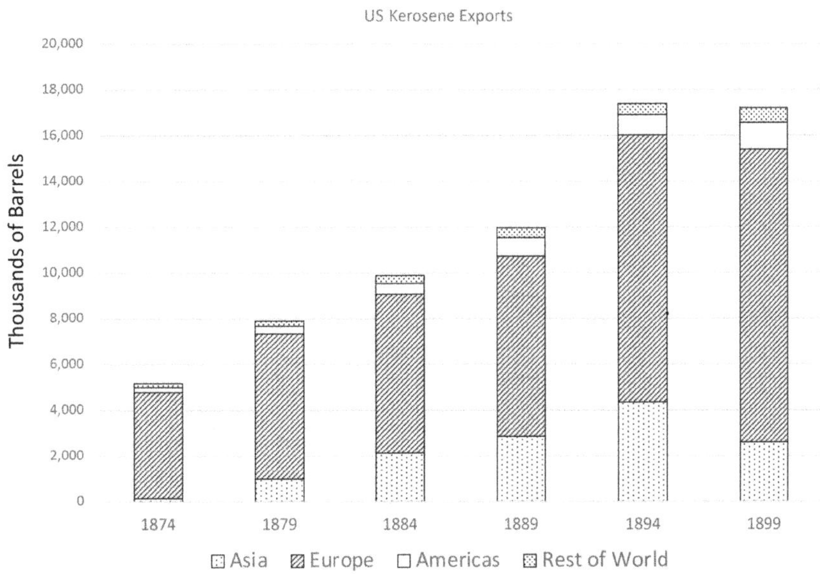

Figure 2.5. US Kerosene Exports, in Thousands of Barrels, for Years at Five-Year Intervals, by Destination. *Source*: From data tabulated in Williamson and Daum (1959, 742–757).

In the period from 1878 to 1880, Azerbaijani production was less than a tenth of the United States (figure 2.6). In 1900, however, Azerbaijan produced nearly half as much kerosene as the United States: 17.3 million barrels (Thompson 1904) compared to about 36.5 million barrels (from oil production data in Day 1922 and estimated volume fractions of refined products in Williamson and Daum 1959, 739). Despite the increasing vibrancy of its oil industry in the late nineteenth century, Azerbaijan was unable to supply the illumination demand in the Russian Empire for much of the period, although imports continually decreased. In the five-year period ending in 1874, the Russian Empire imported 167.2 million barrels of kerosene from the United States. By 1899 imports were negligible, as shown in figure 2.7.

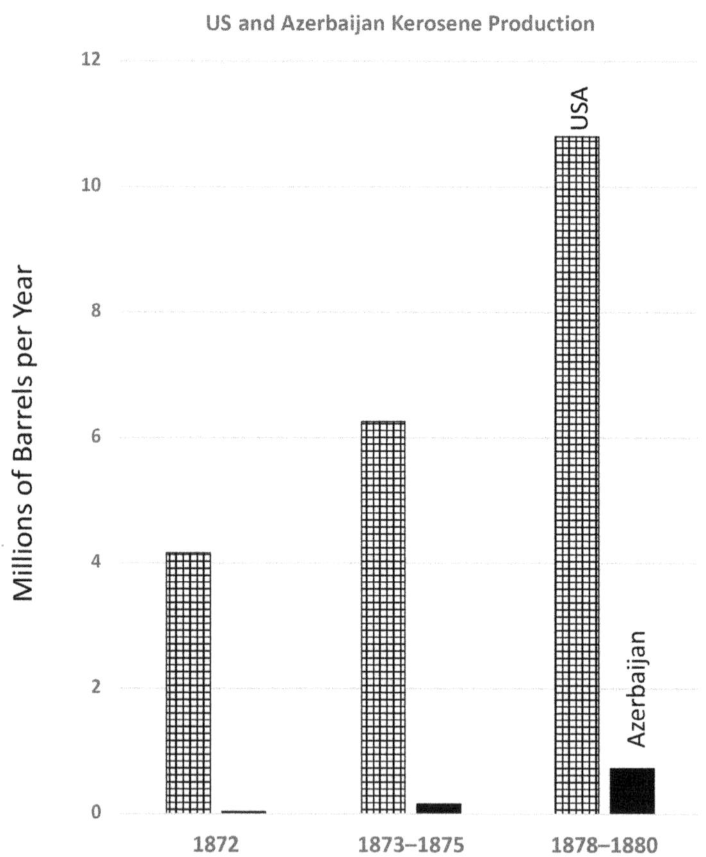

Figure 2.6. US and Azerbaijani Production of Kerosene, 1872–1880. Numbers for 1873–1875 and 1878–1880 are annual averages for the respective time periods.
***Source*: Based on data and estimates in Williamson and Daum (1959, 290, 485, 512).**

Figure 2.7. US Exports of Kerosene to Russia, in Thousands of Forty-Two-Gallon Barrels, for Five-Year Intervals, Showing the Decline as the Azerbaijani Industry Took Over. *Source*: From data tabulated in Williamson and Daum (1959, 742–757).

COMPETING ILLUMINANTS

A number of illuminants other than kerosene were used during the nineteenth century. These included animal fat, wax candles, town gas, camphene, whale oil. We briefly discuss the last three of these, which were sold and used on an industrial scale.

Town Gas

The use of gas for illumination predated the kerosene age. Gas was known in various parts of the world since ancient times, not least in Azerbaijan, with its "temple of the eternal fire" (see chapter 3). Modern gas lighting dates back to the late eighteenth century. One seminal event was Philip Lebon's 1799 French patent for a "thermolampe," a lamp using gas for both illumination and heating purposes. Lebon obtained gas by distillation from wood, but he recognized the possibility of obtaining it from coal. That objective was achieved by the Scottish engineer William Murdoch, who began obtaining gas by heating coal in a retort, beginning in the 1780s. Murdoch also devised ways to distribute gas from a reservoir, and in 1798 he used gas to illuminate a factory in London (Russell 1968, 288).

Frederic Albert Winzer, who anglicized his name to Winsor, emigrated to England from Moravia, then in the Austrian Empire, and formed a company to manufacture and distribute gas for urban illumination. With the help of his highly competent chief engineer, Samuel Clegg, he was able to demonstrate the practicality of street lighting using gas in London. The ideas spread quickly to other places, and by the middle of the nineteenth century, gas lighting of cities was common.

Generally, the gas ("town gas") used in such applications was made from coal. One early case in which the gas was not obtained from coal, but rather from naturally occurring seeps, was that of Fredonia, New York, near the shores of Lake Erie. Natural gas seeps were known along the Canadaway Creek that flowed through the town. A local gunsmith, William Aaron Hart, manually drilled a seventeen-foot-deep well near the creek in 1821 and struck gas, which he was able to distribute to some parts of the town by 1825 using a three-quarter-inch lead pipe (Waples 2005a, 55, 2005b). This was a minor use of gas illumination compared with great cities like London, but since it used naturally occurring gas, it is considered the birth of the natural gas industry in the United States.

One important technical innovation in gas lighting was the Welsbach mantle, invented by Karl Auer von Welsbach in 1887, and perfected by him in 1889. Before around 1885, gas flames obtained their luminosity from incandescent unburned carbon particles, and this resulted in significant soot deposition. In 1855 R.W. Bunsen, Welsbach's professor at Heidelberg, invented a burner that now bears his name, that mixed gas with air before burning, and achieved nearly sootless combustion. A Bunsen flame is pale blue and almost invisible, but when combined with Welsbach's mantle, it made a bright and sootless gas lamp. Welsbach's 1889 mantle was made of a fabric hood impregnated with thorium and cerium oxides. A Bunsen flame would burn off the fabric and heat the oxides to incandescence, giving off a bright white light (Russell 1968, 297).

Camphene

Another major illuminant was called "camphene." This was first developed by A.V.H. Webb of New York City. He devised and patented a process in 1839 to distill turpentine with water and potash to obtain a purified form relatively free of resin. He also patented a lamp to burn the product (Russell 1968, 108). Camphene was reasonably effective as an illuminant, but also produced too much smoke. To make it burn cleaner, it was mixed with alcohol. The resulting diluted form was also called camphene. One serious problem with this form, however, was that it was quite dangerous to burn, on occasion exploding and killing people.

Whale Oil

A nineteenth-century illuminant with different tragic consequences than camphene was whale oil. The term "whale oil" can refer to the oil produced from any whale, or it can refer specifically to the oil produced from the right whale, to distinguish it from "sperm oil" obtained from the sperm whale. Sperm oil was a particularly effective and clean-burning illuminant, but as sperm whales became scarcer, people burned the inferior oil obtained from the right whale. Figure 2.8 shows total whale oil production between 1804 and 1876. Total production of whale oil peaked in 1847. By 1876 it was at around a sixth of the peak level—about the same as in 1820. Kerosene production, in volumetric terms, exceeded whale oil's 1847 peak by 1868 and then rose inexorably.Meanwhile, prices for whale oil in constant dollars peaked in the mid-1850s. Further information can be found in Coleman (1996).

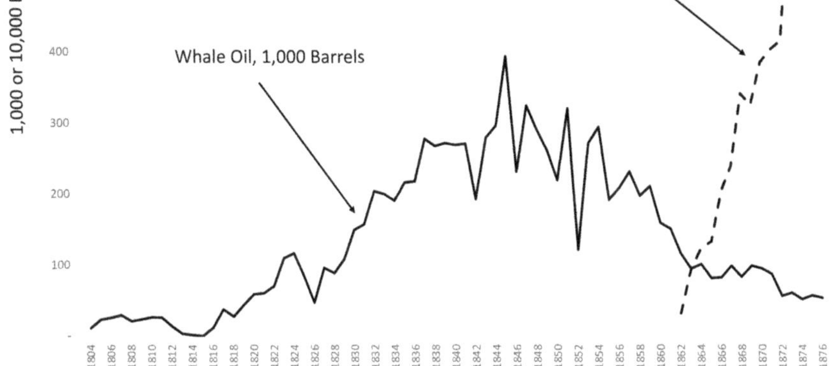

Figure 2.8. US Production of Whale Oil and Kerosene, 1804–1876. Whale oil includes sperm oil and is given in thousands of barrels. Kerosene is given in tens of thousands of barrels. *Source*: Whale oil data are from Starbuck 1878 (Table J, p. 660). Kerosene data are from Williamson and Daum 1959 (Chart 2.1, p. 290, and Table 18.5, p. 485).

COMPARISON OF ILLUMINANTS

Table 2.1, based on a very interesting analysis performed by Nordhaus (1997) and various other sources, provides a comparison of nineteenth-century illuminants with one another and with more modern sources. The price of kerosene, per 1,000 lumen-hours of illumination produced, was 83 cents in 1870 (expressed in constant 2021 dollars). By comparison, camphene in 1855 cost $18.51 2021 dollars per 1,000 lumen-hours, and whale oil cost $10.75 in 1845. Kerosene represented a leap in cost efficiency over both camphene and whale oil. Town gas burned in a lamp with a Welsbach mantle was even more efficient, at only 5 cents (2021 dollars) per 1,000 lumen-hours of illumination in 1890. However, town gas required complex fixed infrastructure and could not reach everywhere as easily as transportable containers of kerosene.

Although kerosene was cost-efficient in terms of price per unit of illumination produced, it was not initially cheap in volumetric terms. In 1856 it cost about a dollar a gallon in money of the day, about the same as lower-quality whale oil from the right whale. It was cheaper than sperm oil ($2.25 per gallon), lard oil ($1.25), and rapeseed oil ($1.25), but more expensive than camphene (63 cents) (Brice 2002, 78). However, given the dangers posed by burning camphene, and kerosene's superiority as an illuminant, it won out over camphene as well.

DID PETROLEUM SAVE THE WHALES?

Given that kerosene replaced whale oil as an illuminant, it is fair to ask whether the petroleum industry saved the whales from extinction in the nineteenth century. Some commentators have answered in the affirmative (e.g., Meyer 2010; Brice 2010). Others (e.g., Smaje 2020) fervently deny the proposition and make the further point that whaling in the present day is enabled by the petroleum products powering the ships. Both sides have a point, and the truth of the matter is complicated. Abundant kerosene from petroleum certainly made burning whale oil much less necessary. However, whaling had already peaked two decades before the oil boom of the 1860s. Even before the oil boom, camphene was a cheaper substitute for whale oil and had increased its share of the illumination market from very low levels in 1850 to nearly 9 percent in 1860, even with the emerging competition from kerosene. The petroleum industry probably did help the whales, but it would be stretching the point to say that it alone saved them from extinction.

Table 2.1. Illumination Sources

Light Source	*Typical Lumens*	*Efficiency (Lumens/Watt)*	*Approximate Date for Price*	*Price, $US per 1000 lumen-hours (money of the Day)*	*Price, $US per 1000 lumen-hours (2021 money)*	*Labor Price (hours of work per 1000 lumen hours)*	*Share of the Lighting Market in 1850*	*Share of the Lighting Market in 1860*
Wax Candle	~13	0.0757	1800	$0.400	$8.67	5.37	Small	Small
Whale oil lamp	~15	0.1343	1845	$0.300	$10.75	4.9	65.50%	19.40%
Camphene lamp	~15	0.0575	1855	$0.590	$18.51	5.94	~0	8.90%
Kerosene lamp	~20	0.159	1870	$0.035	$0.83	0.2253	~0	20.30%
Kerosene lamp, modern Coleman	45	0.3651	1993	$0.103	$0.19	0.0098	na	na
Town Gas, Welsbach mantle	Hundreds	0.5914	1890	$0.002	$0.05	0.083	16%	38%
Electric filament lightbulb, 100 W	1200	12	1980	$0.004	$0.01	0.000678	na	na

Notes: Illumination figures and prices are from Nordhaus 1997. Prices are for luminous output and should not be confused with the price of the fuel per gallon. 2021 prices are estimated using Webster 2021. Market shares in 1850 and 1860 are from Kaiser 2017. Market shares do not add up to 100% because other illumination sources such as rosin, cottonseed oil, lard, and others are not represented here. Illumination and prices for town gas are for town gas used in a lamp with a Welsbach Mantle. However, market shares of town gas in 1850 and 1860 are for gas without reference to the Welsbach Mantle, which was not invented until 1889.

Chapter 3

Before the Nineteenth Century

Before continuing our discussion of the nineteenth-century oil industry in the United States and Azerbaijan, we take a step back and explore the occurrence and exploitation of oil in those countries in previous time periods.

AZERBAIJAN

Azerbaijan has had an oil trade since ancient times. Plutarch, the ancient Greek historian who described the campaigns of Alexander the Great, describes troops using oil from the Absheron peninsula for illumination in the fourth century BCE, transporting it in waterskins or clay vessels. Arab geographer Masoudi described white (light) Surakhani oil and Surakhani "eternal fires," or burning gas seeps, in the tenth century.

Eternal Fires

Seeps of inflammable gas were used in religious worship by Zoroastrians. Fire worshippers' temples on the Absheron peninsula date back to the sixth century BCE. The Surakhani fire worshippers' temple and other similar ones were destroyed by Alexander and later by the Byzantine emperor Irakly in 624. In 636 the temple was restored by local fire worshippers, with help from Persian exiles. The temple was destroyed again during the Arab invasion of Azerbaijan in 643. In the seventeenth century, the temple was restored yet again using funds from Indian merchants who lived in the Surakhani area. This is confirmed by the ancient Hindi inscriptions found on the flagstone of the temple and deciphered by Indian scholars.

Samuel Gottlieb Gmelin, a Russian scientist who visited Baku in 1770 on behalf of the Saint-Petersburg Academy of Sciences, wrote: "Local fire worshippers . . . are the descendants of ancient grebes [Zoroastrians], who survived in Persia after Islam was established there. They worship their inextinguishable fire as something very sacred. . . . Those devout people from India visit this fire in Baku for salvation. . . . One of these Temples is still standing near the Surakhani settlement" (Mir-Babayev 2008, 8). The restored temple still stands today.

A Medieval and Early Modern Pre-Nineteenth-Century Oil Industry

Various accounts, some of which are detailed below, paint a picture of a thriving pre-nineteenth-century oil industry in what is today Azerbaijan. Approximately 120 hand-dug wells, ranging in depth from 14 to 140 feet, were operating at various times in the Absheron peninsula settlements arrayed around Baku: Balakhani, Surakhani, Bibi-Eibat, Binagadi, Sabunchi, Romani, and Shubani, with a large part of the oil concentrated in Balakhani. Operators relied on oil seeping spontaneously into the wells. As some of the following accounts outline, oil was gathered in buckets and lifted out, often with the aid of animal power. Oil was both used locally and exported. Wells were exploited until the seeps stopped. Often, oil would begin accumulating again in an idle well after some time had passed, at which point exploitation would resume.

Some Known Wells

A noteworthy medieval oil well was the one dug by Allahyar Mamedali Nur Ogli in Balakhani in 1594, to a depth of 115 feet. In Balakhani local residents found inscriptions on stones in 1823 recounting how one well, the Khalafi well, had been renovated 200 years before. Other old wells, constructed in the eighteenth century, included Chambu, Haji Zurabi, Dostakov, Salakhi, Urusi, Kazy, Shakh-Safi, Aghai, Ali-Beyi, Hasan-Ali, Khanali, and Irzagouli. These were renovated even before Azerbaijan's entry into the Russian Empire.

Accounts of Travelers and Observers

Various travelers since the eighth century have visited the Caucasus and have noted in their chronicles that the political and economic life of the Absheron peninsula was closely tied to oil. Masoudi wrote in the tenth century of Absheron's black (heavy) and white (light) oils and their export to Turkey and other countries. Marco Polo described the use of oil on the Absheron for medicinal purposes and for lighting in 1273. He also confirmed the export of oil from Baku to the countries of the Middle East. At the beginning of the thirteenth century, Mohammed Bekran, an Arab historian who visited the Absheron peninsula, wrote of oil extraction from hand-dug wells in Balakhani. Another observer, Amin Ahmet ar-Razi, who visited Absheron in 1601, noted that black and white oils were being extracted from nearly 500 wells.

In 1636, Adam Elschleger, a German diplomat and traveler, known also as Olearius, described the oil wells he saw:

> Those different wells numbering up to 30 are located at a distance of one rifle shot [from Baku]; a strong oil fountain emerges from these wells. [There] were three main wells . . . two sazhens [fourteen feet] in depth. . . . several crossbeams were installed which could be used as stairs. . . . Here, it was possible to dredge either black or white oil out of the well, but the first was more abundant than the second (Mir-Babayev 2008, 10).

J. Hanvey, one of the directors of the English-Russian trading company, visited Baku one hundred years after Olearius. He noted that Baku residents used gas for cooking food, boiling water, and making lime. He also noted that Surakhani white oil was considered very valuable and exported to various countries: it was touted as a remedy for kidney stones, chest pains, convulsions, and other ailments (Mir-Babayev 2008, 10).

E. Kempfer, the secretary of the Swedish Embassy in Persia, who was in Baku from January 6 to 8, 1683 wrote the following:

> A countless number of tight vertical wells are dug for oil extraction. Oil [flows] inside these wells in abundance and permanency. . . . The solid clay soil allows deep digging to the desired layers without installing any walls and posing no danger to the lives of the diggers. Extraction of oil from the wells is done using skin buckets manually or by means of . . . [a] special mechanism which is put in motion by two horses running in a circle. . . . Here, work never stops except . . . at night. . . . Oil is transported in skin cylinders on four-wheeled carts, to the cities of Shemakha and Baku; from the first point, it goes on camels within the country's boundaries, but the second point serves [for sea] transport to Girkania, Uzbek and Cherkask oblast and Dagestan (BakIzv 1883).

In 1733, during an interlude when the Absheron peninsula was controlled by Russia, Ioann Lerkh of the Russian Embassy in Persia noted the following after visiting the Baku oil region:

> I have passed five versts (3,500 feet) from [the] inextinguishable fire to Balakhani up to the black oil springs. . . . During the [time of the] Persian Shah, there were 52 such wells. . . . Wells with depths of 20 sazhens [140 feet] were

> known as strong oil fountains [yielding] 500 batmans [roughly 35 barrels] of oil every day. . . . Oil from these wells flows into big deep holes and [is] then transported in big skin bags put on carts to Baku. The rest of the oil is poured into three holes or cellars, and . . . sold in Gilan, Shemakha and other places. Some remaining oil is used in the city (Mir-Babayev 2008, 11).

In 1771, the above-mentioned S.G. Gmelin reported on what he saw during his visit to Baku:

> [W]ells are closed with stones separated by pieces of clay where you can see the carved name of the Khan of Baku. It shows that no one can take any oil from this well until the Khan's guards open the wells for use. It was reported by local residents that the revenues of the Baku Khan from salt and oil sales were equal in revenue to 35 to 40 thousand rubles. One pood [36.1 pounds] of salt costs 7 or 8 kopecks while one batman of black oil, which is equal to 15 pounds when used for burning, costs 5 kopecks (Gmelin 1771).

Gmelin's account is confirmed by A. Yartsev, who went to Baku before it became a part of Russia again in the nineteenth century. In particular, Yartsev wrote in 1812:

> One Baku Prince has the right to sell all mountainous oil from this country. [Oil] is in strong abundance in Balakhani. [It] is transported to the city of Baku. In that city, there are no special warehouses for sales operations; but there are 15 wells outside the city dug in the very solid gypsum stone and [lined with] stones inside. The reserve oil is poured into these wells and stored [until] it is sold by merchants (Pazhitnov 1940, 11)

The description given by Marschall von Bieberstein, who visited Baku in 1796, is also interesting: "The Absheron peninsula is rich with inexhaustible volumes of oil. . . . The main market for oil is Gilan because those who cultivate silkworms in this province believe . . . that the oil is the only thing which can be burnt for lighting houses without causing any harm to insects" (Mir-Babayev 2008, 12).

UNITED STATES

Compared with Azerbaijan, the United States did not have an organized petroleum trade in medieval and ancient times, at least not one known to us. However, Native Americans in the territory of what is now the United States were aware of petroleum seeps and used the oil in various ways—for example, as a sealant or as a medical salve. European settlers had also begun exploiting oil in similar ways by the beginning of the nineteenth century.

New York

Owen (1975, 8–9) gives a comprehensive account of the occurrence and early exploitation of oil seeps in Pennsylvania and New York. What follows in this section is based in part on his treatment. Jesuit missionaries reached Cayuga Lake in 1656 and were told about an oil spring near present-day Cuba, New York, by Native Americans. Ash (2016) discusses earlier (1627) writings of Friar Joseph de la Roche Daillon purportedly describing the spring and raises considerable doubts about whether Friar Daillon really traveled far south enough to see it, or whether what he was describing was really petroleum.

It is worth noting that the Cuba Spring was not far from the location of the future giant Bradford Oil Field, which is mostly in Pennsylvania but extends into New York State. A 1670 map by the missionary René de Bréchant de Galinée shows the spring as "Fontaine de bitumen." Galinée also observed a natural gas spring west of Canandaigua Lake in 1669 on an expedition with the explorer Robert Cavalier, Sieur de La Salle. Petroleum from the Cuba Spring was a valuable trade commodity used for medicinal purposes. Benjamin Silliman Sr. published an account of the Cuba Spring in 1833. Silliman Sr. was the father of the Benjamin Silliman Jr. who analyzed the oil of the Pennsylvania Rock Oil Company in 1855 (see chapters 4 and 7).

Pennsylvania

The petroleum seeps of northwestern Pennsylvania, which would eventually point the way to the modern oil industry in the United States, were known to Native Americans and attracted the interest of many European observers. Native Americans dug pits into which the oil seeped and collected. They lined the pits with logs cut using stone axes. The pits were noticed by early European settlers and can still be seen today. Archaeological work has revealed that pits not far from the site of Drake's 1859 well were worked sometime between 1415 and 1440 (Pees 2002, 34). Later settlers observed Native Americans using oil for medicinal and other purposes.

Peter Kalm, a former student of the great Swedish scientist Linnaeus, visited the Oil Creek area in 1748 and described the oil springs there. Oil Creek also appeared as a source of petroleum on Lewis Evans's 1755 map of colonial America, as it did in a 1778 topographic and resource map by Thomas Hutchins. The Revolutionary War general Benjamin Lincoln reported in 1783 that his troops used Oil Creek petroleum medicinally, specifically treating rheumatism, and as a purgative (Owen 1975, 9).

Western Virginia and Washington's Will

The first scouts of European descent to explore the wilderness of western Virginia, in the territory of what is now West Virginia, noticed oil and gas springs. No less a personage than George Washington, the first president of the United States, learned of such springs when he was fighting with the Virginia Regiment in the French and Indian War during the 1750s. Later, in 1770, Washington visited the lands that would eventually become the locus of the West Virginia oil industry, in the valley of the Ohio River between present-day Parkersburg and Charleston. He was to be paid in wilderness land for his service in the French and Indian War and was evaluating candidate areas. He traveled up the Great Kanawha River and was told of a burning spring near present-day Malden, West Virginia. Although he did not visit the site of the spring, he decided to take title to 250 acres surrounding it. He left the spring to the public in his will, noting "The tract of which the 123 acres is a moiety, was taken up by General Andrew Lewis and myself for and on account of a bituminous spring which is contained, of so inflamiable [sic] a nature as to burst forth as freely as spirits, and is nearly as difficult to extinguish" (McKain and Allen 1994, 2). There is a marker, erected in 1963 by the West Virginia Oil and Natural Gas Industry Centennial Committee, near the site of the spring (Historic Marker Database 2022).

Besides Washington's spring, others were "discovered" by European settlers (they were already known to Native Americans). Wilderness scout Jesse Hughes found one about eighty miles north, near present-day Parkersburg, around the same time as Washington was visiting the region. The spring was on a creek near the Little Kanawha River; Hughes named the creek "Burning Spring Run." Another Founding Father of the United States, Thomas Jefferson, knew of this spring and described how the escaping gas could be lit on fire in 1781 (WVGES 2004). According to McKain and Allen (1994, 2), a Dr. J.P. Hale reported that Native Americans were exploiting oil seeps in the Kanawha River Valley in the 1750s. In addition, oil was struck in 1790 near present-day Elizabeth, West Virginia, by drillers who were trying to find water (McKain and Allen 1994, 2).

Ohio

An oil spring was discovered by early scouts of the Ohio River near Macksburg, Ohio, in 1787, not far from the future cradle of the Ohio petroleum industry. Native Americans used and traded the oil in the region (Camp 2016).

Oklahoma

Oil seeps were known to Native Americans in the territory that is now Oklahoma, and several non-Native observers reported on them in the early and mid-nineteenth century. Sorenson (2009) provides a comprehensive account, which we now paraphrase closely. The first report was by Lieutenant T.B. Wheelock (1834), who was with the Dragoon Regiment led by Colonel Henry Dodge on the first US military expedition through the Wichita Mountains: "passed several springs of rock oil, (petroleum)" (Wheelock 1834, 375, quoted in Sorenson 2009, 84). The seeps were most likely located near the present-day Loco and Headton oil fields. In 1845, Lieutenant A.R. Johnston of Fort Washita reported oil in the northern Arbuckle Mountains seeping from a steeply dipping sandstone. In multiple reports from 1845 to 1853, Chickasaw Indian agents wrote that at least two oil springs in southern Oklahoma were used by Native Americans for medicinal purposes (Sorenson 2009, 87–88). And in 1852, Captain Randolph B. Marcy, while returning from an expedition to find the source of the Red River, which forms part of the boundary between Oklahoma and Texas, reported oil seeps near Medicine Bluffs (Sorenson 2009, 90–91).

Texas

Signs of oil have long been noticed in Texas. The first recording of an observation was made by Luis de Moscoso, a survivor of the De Soto expedition. In July 1543 members of the expedition noticed oil floating on the surface of the water between Sabine Pass and High Island. They gathered some and used it to caulk their ships (Olien 1995). There was also a well-known oil spring at Sour Lake, where a gusher would be drilled in 1902. This was only one of many long-attested seeps along the Gulf coast (Owen 1975, 8). A seep at Oil Springs was long known by Native Americans, who used the oil medicinally. Non-Native settlers learned of the seep and by around 1790 were using the oil as a lubricant for their wagons, as well as a salve for their animals (Folsom 1995). The Oil Springs seep guided the drilling of the Barret well, the first modern oil well in Texas (see chapter 5).

California

California's Native Americans were aware of oil seeps and used material from tar pools to caulk their boats, help make arrows and baskets, and many other purposes (Hodgson 2003; Henderson 2001). Such pools were observed by Spaniards as early as the 1500s. Writing in 1775, Don Pedro Fages observed that at "the foot of the range which runs toward the west, on the road lying between the Rio de la Porciuncula and the Ojo del Agua de los Alisos, the scouts found pools of bitumen bubbling [out of the ground]" (Fages 1775). Tar pools still exist in the city of Los Angeles, where the La Brea Tar Pits are a famous attraction.

Chapter 4

The First Modern Oil Well

Who drilled the first modern oil well? The question is not as easy to answer as it sounds, and the answer depends to a large extent on definitions. Edwin Drake's 1859 well near Titusville, Pennsylvania, has often been cited as the first modern oil well (e.g., Yergin 1991). However, there were contemporaneous and earlier efforts elsewhere.

What makes a nineteenth-century oil well recognizably "modern"? There are a number of factors to consider, summarized also in table 4.1:

- Was the well deliberately created to search for oil?
- Was there an associated oil company?
- Was the well drilled using a specialized apparatus, or was it dug by hand?
- Was the drilling mechanized, or did it depend on human or animal power?
- Was the borehole cased?
- Did the well touch off a boom in the oil business?

Let us consider some notable early oil wells of the nineteenth century in light of these factors.

HAND-DUG OIL WELLS

Azerbaijani Wells before 1846

As we have observed in chapter 3, the exploitation of oil in Azerbaijan has been going on since ancient times. In the nineteenth century this ancient activity was extended, with old wells being exploited and some new ones being dug. In 1803 Kasimbey Mansurbekov of Baku dug two wells in Bibi-Eibat

Bay, eighteen and thirty meters off the Absheron peninsula; this was the first-known exploitation of offshore oil. The wells were protected from the water by an enclosure made of tightly knit wooden planks (Mir-Babayev 2021). German traveler Eduard Eichwald (1834) published a description of an ongoing operation he observed in 1825 near the village of Surakhani on the same peninsula, collecting naturally seeping oil. The sixteen wells were hand dug, lined with stone, and covered to prevent evaporation. One well, named Mustafa, was about twenty-seven feet deep and produced oil at a maximum rate of about 1.5 gallons per day.

Azerbaijan is the only known country in the world with oil production data available before the late 1850s. The data are incomplete and not to the same standard of accuracy as statistics published after 1862. However, they do provide a picture of a consistent and thriving preindustrial oil trade from hand-dug wells. Estimates of Azerbaijani oil production were compiled by Pazhitnov (1940). They are given in table D.2, and plotted in figure 4.1. Production mostly hovered between 25,000 and 30,000 barrels per year. To put this in perspective, note that by 1900, Azerbaijan was producing 30,000 barrels of oil approximately every three and a half hours!

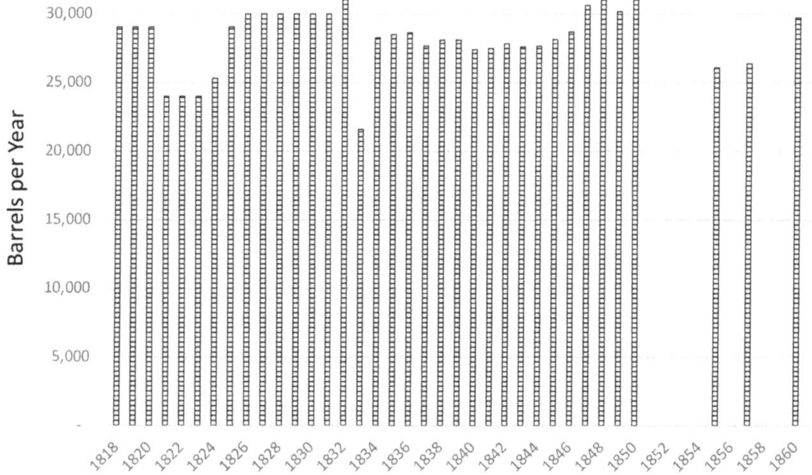

Figure 4.1. Azerbaijani Oil Production before 1862. ***Source*****: Calculated from estimates published in Pazhitnov (1940), assuming 8.3374 poods per barrel. Also given in table D.2. A gap does not imply zero production; it simply indicates missing data.**

The 1850 Pico Wells, California

Andrés Pico served as the Mexican acting governor of Alta California in 1847 and was later a state legislator after California became a US state. Beginning in 1850, he collected crude oil from seeps found in the Pico Canyon, named for his family, in present-day Los Angeles County. He distilled the crude to create illuminating oil for the San Fernando Mission. Pico's wells were hand dug, not drilled (Prutzman 1913, 159).

It is worth noting that later in the century, Pico Canyon became important in establishing the California oil industry, as discussed in chapter 5. However, these later developments cannot be considered direct descendants of Andrés Pico's operations in 1850, except perhaps in the sense that Pico's work showed there was exploitable oil in the area.

Ignacy Łukasiewicz, Austria-Hungary

In Bóbrka, Galicia, then in the Austro-Hungarian Empire, Jan Zeh, Ignacy Łukasiewicz, and others developed methods for refining crude oil into a usable illumination oil, probably close to kerosene, and a suitable lamp for burning the refined product. On July 31, 1853, the Lvov General Hospital became the first public building in the world lit by petroleum lamps, and in 1858–1859 the Emperor Ferdinand Northern Railway converted to petroleum illumination. In the early years, oil was obtained from hand-dug pits. Drilling equipment was introduced to the area in 1863 (Sozanski et al. 2006; Frank 2005).

Łukasiewicz performed very important early work in refining, but his hand-dug pits cannot be considered modern oil wells.

Mehedinţeanu Brothers, Romania

In 1856 and 1857, the brothers Theodor and Marin Mehedinţeanu refined oil gathered from new and preexisting hand-dug pits in the Ploieşti area of Romania. These cannot be considered modern oil wells in any sense. Nevertheless, the Mehedinţeanu brothers began producing kerosene to light the streets of Bucharest in December 1856, soon ramping up to seventy-five tons a day (Dimancescu 2020).

James Miller Williams, Canada

In 1858, in the area around present-day Oil Springs, Ontario, James Miller Williams dug for bitumen by hand and found crude oil as well. Sometime between 1854 and 1857, Williams had acquired the International Mining and

Manufacturing Company, a financially unsuccessful company that had been established by Henry and Charles Nelson Tripp in 1854 to produce asphalt from the Eniskillen gum beds. By 1858, Williams was already refining crude oil to produce kerosene. As in the case of the Romanian and Austro-Hungarian wells mentioned above, Miller's hand-dug pits cannot be considered modern oil wells.

It is possible that sometime during 1859, Williams drilled a 146-foot well using a spring pole apparatus. *The Globe*, quoted by (Gray 2008a, 24), reported on September 6, 1861, that the well had "been in operation two years."

DRILLED SALT WELLS THAT FOUND OIL

The 1806–1808 Ruffner Well, Western Virginia

Beginning in 1806 and continuing to 1808, David and Joseph Ruffner drilled a fifty-eight-foot salt well near the Kanawha River, near present-day Charleston, West Virginia, and discovered oil along with the brine. The Ruffners were working at a site not far George Washington's burning spring (McKain and Allen 1994, 2). They used a spring pole, described in chapter 7. They also used a hollow wooden tube as rudimentary casing in their hole.

The 1814 and 1816 Caldwell, Ohio Wells

In 1814 Robert McKee and Silas Thorla drilled a well looking for salt near what is now Caldwell, Ohio. Like the Ruffners, they used a spring pole. At a depth of approximately 200 feet, they found brine, oil, and gas. Another well two years later yielded the same results. The oil was initially an undesirable by-product, but McKee and Thorla eventually extracted value from it by selling it as a patent medicine (Camp 2016, 22; McKain and Allen 1994, 2).

Samuel P. Hildreth (1826) wrote about these wells and about petroleum in southeastern Ohio and western Virginia more generally. He wrote:

> [T]he petroleum affords considerable profit and is beginning to be in demand for workshops and manufactories: It affords a clear, brisk light, when burned in this way, and will be a valuable article for lighting the street lamps in the future cities of Ohio. Since the first settlement of the regions west of the Appalachian range the hunters and pioneers have been acquainted with this oil. . . . [I]t soon arrested their attention and acquired great value in the eyes of the simple sons of the forest. From its success in rheumatism, burns, coughs, sprains etc., it was justly entitled to its celebrity.

In a later article, Hildreth (1833) wrote of the superior lubricating properties of petroleum compared to animal and vegetable oils.

The 1818, 1820, and 1829 Kentucky Wells

Martin Beatty of Virginia, an iron-furnace operator, decided to try drilling for salt in nearby southeastern Kentucky, near the Tennessee border. He contracted with Marcus Huling and Andrew Zimmerman to do the drilling, and they completed a well on December 4, 1818. They used a spring pole, drilling to a depth of 170 feet, and striking oil along with salt water. The well flowed roughly 100 barrels of oil per day. Beatty was disappointed, but Huling and Zimmerman decided to try and sell the oil, transporting it by river in barrels. Huling claimed to have sent 2,000 barrels to Europe (Nuttall 2014, 70; Sorenson 2020, 86).

In 1820 a Captain G.W. Hunt drilled for salt in the southwestern tip of Clinton County, Kentucky, in the southern part of the state. He struck oil, which made the brine unsuitable for salt production. The well also flowed gas, which could be lit to produce a flame twenty feet high. None of the oil was marketed (Nuttall 2014, 71).

In 1829 yet another salt well struck oil, more spectacularly. The Old American Well, sometimes called the Great American Well, was drilled manually by kicking down a four-inch bit on the Lemuel Stockton Farm in southern Kentucky, near the Tennessee border. Drilling was directed by one Colonel Emerson. On March 11 the drillers struck oil at a depth of 175 feet. The well flowed over a hundred barrels of oil per hour, rising in a fountain twelve to fourteen feet above the ground, and forming a forty- to fifty-mile slick on the Cumberland River. It was set on fire by a young boy and burned for three weeks. The oil was marketed and even influenced pioneering refiner Samuel Kier (see chapters 5 and 7). Kier's wife had developed tuberculosis and been prescribed oil from the well. This stimulated Kier to begin selling oil from his own salt wells (Nuttall 2014, 71–73; Sorenson 2020, 87).

The 1842 Rathbone Well, Western Virginia

William P. Rathbone and his sons John C. and John V. Rathbone purchased land in the Burning Springs area of western Virginia. They began a variety of businesses, including a grist mill, a boat yard, and a general store. They also sold oil seeping into an 1835 salt well that someone else had drilled on the property before they acquired it. They sold the oil as a medicine. In 1842 they decided to drill for salt. They hired drillers Silas Reynolds and A.P. Gay from the Kanawha salt works, to deepen a different salt well that had been on the property since 1832. On June 24, 1842, the drillers struck salt and oil at 300 feet. They sold the new oil as a medicine for several years (McKain and Allen 1994, 9).

George Lemon, Western Virginia

In the early 1850s, George Lemon drilled wells along the Hughes River, about twenty miles west of Parkersburg, then in western Virginia, but today in the state of West Virginia. Lemon may have been drilling only for salt when he found oil, but he may have been looking for either salt or oil; it is not clear. His drilling apparatus was water powered (McKain and Allen 1994, 5).

The 1859 Ross Well, Oklahoma

The first-known oil-producing well in Oklahoma was in 1859, forty-eight years before the territory became a state. The well, near what is now Salina, in Mayes County, had been created in a search for salt by Lewis Ross, brother of Cherokee chief John Ross. According to Skelton (2006), the well was drilled, while Sorenson (2009) says it was dug by hand. The accidentally discovered oil was sold for use in lamps.

WELLS DRILLED FOR OIL

The 1846 Baku Well

The 1846 Baku well has a good claim on being the world's first modern industrial oil well. Western literature has mostly ignored it, but it has been chronicled by Mir-Babayev (2011, 2017, 2021) and Matveichuk (2002, 2004). Matveichuk (2002) gives the year of the well as 1848, but the research detailed in the Mir-Babayev papers establishes it as 1846.

The story of the 1846 well began years earlier, with a talented Russian engineer named Nikolai Voskoboinikov who was working in the Baku area. On January 1, 1825, an order from Yegor Kankrin, Russia's finance minister, placed all oil wells under the control of the state. As a major in the Bakinskii Corps of Mining Engineers, Voskoboinikov was placed in charge of oil fields and salt mines in Baku and Shirvan. He made a number of innovations. In 1835 he developed a canvas ventilator to feed fresh air into an oil well and make maintenance easier and safer. In 1836 and 1837, he organized a storage and supply system for oil in the Baku area. In 1834 he designed, built, and operated a refinery to produce a kerosene-like illuminating oil from crude oil; we provide more details in chapter 7.

Voskoboinikov recognized the inefficiency of large hand-dug pits and was an early proponent of deliberate drilling for oil. He began developing his ideas in the late 1830s, two decades before Edwin Drake's well in Pennsylvania. However, he had difficulty generating interest for his proposals, especially since he was distracted by unjust accusations that he stole oil from the existing operations in Baku. A royal commission sent to investigate the allegations exonerated him in 1838. He was transferred to the Department of Geological Engineers of the Caucasus and in 1841 became a colonel.

In 1843 Voskoboinikov met Vasili Semyonov, an enlightened member of the Caucasus executive council, in Tiflis, Georgia. Semyonov took an interest in Voskoboinikov's ideas and worked with him to produce a report. Semyonov submitted Report 99, dated December 22, 1844, under his own name. He did this not to steal credit but to maximize the chances of the report's acceptance by the upper levels of government. Semyonov noted that annual revenues from black oil sales ranged from 80,000 to 85,000 silver rubles, but these sums could be raised to 100,000, if a number of actions were taken, including rebuilding existing hand-dug wells, drilling for oil following Voskoboinikov's proposal, creating a precipitation tank for separating oil from water, and ensuring conditions for oil refining (DMS 1844). The report was approved initially by the commander of the Trans-Caucasian region, Adjutant General Aleksandr Ivanovich Neidhardt Grand Duke Mikhail Vorontsov, the tsar's new governor general of the Caucasus, saw Semyonov's report and authorized 1,000 rubles in silver for oil drilling, disbursed on April 30, 1845.

The drilling effort, which occurred in the Bibi-Eibat area, fell under the supervision of Voskoboinikov's successor in the Bakinskii Corps of Mining Engineers, Major Alexeev. Success was reported on July 14, 1846. The well was sixty-nine feet deep (ACAC 1885, 145). Grand Duke Mikhail Vorontsov reported the success of the well in his address to Fyodor Pavlovich Vronchenko, state secretary, dated July 8–14, 1847. "I authorized the Shemakha Public Chamber to conduct oil exploration work in Baku uyezd [district], on the shore of the Caspian, in Beybad [Bibi-Eibat] tract using earth augers at the basis of required fees to the amount of 1000 rubles in silver allocated by you in 1845 for this purpose. [Following this,] the acting Director of Baku and Shirvan mineral fields reported that they had tapped . . . oil in Beybad" (ACAC 1884, 137). Although the well was in the Bibi-Eibat area, it is not considered the discovery well of the main Bibi-Eibat field; that well was not drilled until 1871.

Today a monument stands at the location of the original 1846 well, not far from downtown Baku, featuring a reconstruction of the derrick.

The 1859 Hazlett Well, Western Virginia

In early to mid-1859, Robert W. Hazlett successfully drilled for oil at Oil Spring Run, near the town of Petroleum in present-day West Virginia. It is not known if his drilling equipment was mechanized, but his well was drilled explicitly for oil, under the auspices of a dedicated associated company (McKain and Allen 1994, 11). Hazlett's well was roughly contemporaneous with Drake's.

The 1859 Drake Well, Pennsylvania

The story of the Drake well is told in great detail in countless sources, among them Yergin's (1991) popular and fascinating history of oil and especially the dedicated book on Drake by Brice (2009). What follows is a brief summary of the main points.

We begin with George Henry Bissell, founder of the Pennsylvania Rock Oil Company, perhaps the world's first truly modern oil company. It was Bissell's vision that eventually led to the drilling of the Edwin Drake well. George Henry Bissell was born on November 8, 1821, in Hanover, New Hampshire. He graduated from Dartmouth College in 1845, after which he held a number of jobs, including journalist, high school principal, and professor of languages. While working, he also studied law, obtaining a degree and gaining admission to the New York bar in 1853. He then began practicing law in New York City.

Bissell passed through the oil regions of western Pennsylvania on a trip to the Northeast from New Orleans, where he worked as an educator in the 1840s, and became interested in the surface seeps of oil. His interest grew when he happened to see a sample of Pennsylvania oil on a visit to Dartmouth. The sample had been brought to the medical school there in 1853 for analysis by Francis Beattie Brewer, a Massachusetts physician who was also a Dartmouth alumnus. Two years earlier, Brewer had moved to Titusville, Pennsylvania, to join his father's lumber firm, Brewer, Watson, and Company, and had there also become intrigued by the seeps of oil on the company's land.

Bissell's New York law partner Jonathan C. Eveleth went to Pennsylvania to investigate the oil-bearing lands near Titusville from which the Dartmouth sample had come. The Brewer, Watson, land was mostly in Venango County, between high mountains in the valley of Oil Creek. It included the Hibbard farm. Bissell and Eveleth bought or leased about 1,200 acres of land from Brewer, Watson, for $5,000. On December 30, 1854, they established the Pennsylvania Rock Oil Company of New York, which intended initially to produce oil from surface seeps or via hand-dug wells.

Bissell later had the idea of drilling for oil. Allegedly, the idea came to him in 1856 after he saw an advertisement for rock oil medicine that had a picture of drilling derricks that were used to drill for salt. Some petroleum used for medicinal purposes was a by-product of salt drilling. Pennsylvania oil was marketed as a patent medicine, notably by Samuel Kier. Similar activities were occurring in neighboring western Virginia. Kier and others believed oil could be useful as an illuminant, and Bissell had reached a similar conclusion. Neither idea—drilling for oil deliberately or using petroleum as an illuminant—was actually original, as we have discussed, although Bissell may not have known it.

Needing more capital for the company, Bissell attempted to interest a group of investors from New Haven, Connecticut. They were cautious. An analysis of an oil sample by Benjamin Silliman, Jr. of nearby Yale University helped convince them. In 1855 Silliman issued his "Report on the Rock Oil, or Petroleum from Venango Co., Pennsylvania, with Special Reference to Its Use for Illumination and Other Purposes"—which is perhaps one of the most consequential reports ever issued by a scientific consultant. The New Haven investors, among them James Townsend, president of the City Savings Bank, agreed to buy stock if the company was restructured under Connecticut law, which was more liberal than that of Pennsylvania. The Pennsylvania Rock Oil Company of Connecticut was formed on September 18, 1855, with a capitalization of $300,000. The company acquired all the lands owned by Bissell and Eveleth that showed oil, and it leased the rest for ninety-nine years. The amount paid is not certain but is believed to have been $24,000.

Conflicts soon arose between Bissell and Eveleth on the one hand and the New Haven group on the other. Bissell wanted to move fast, and the New Haven investors were conservative and parsimonious. The company did little in 1855 and 1856. Bissell and Eveleth convinced the New Haven investors to buy some of their stock, promising to find another party to work the prospect. On November 6, 1856, the property was leased to David H. Lyman and Rensellaer Havens of New York. However, the following year was a depression year, with collapsing commodity prices. Lyman and Havens were able to back out of their lease. Some of the New Haven group unjustly accused Bissell of having devised nothing more than an elaborate scheme to unload some of his shares. Bissell and Eveleth attempted a reconciliation, suggesting the formation of a new company. The New Haven investors were not interested. Townsend and others from New Haven acquired more stock and gradually marginalized Bissell and Eveleth. They organized a new company, the Seneca Oil Company, to take up the lease that Lyman and Havens had abandoned.

In 1858 Townsend employed Edwin Drake to drill for oil on behalf of Seneca. Edwin Laurentine Drake was born March 29, 1819 in Greenville, New

York, and grew up in Castleton Corners, Vermont. He held several different jobs before becoming a conductor for the New York and New Haven Railroad. In 1857 he fell ill and resigned from that job, settling in New Haven to recuperate. During this period he bought some shares of stock in the Seneca Oil Company. Drake accepted a job with Seneca to travel to Titusville and report on the site to the stockholders. He made a brief trip in December 1857 and reported positively, having witnessed the skimming of oil from Oil Creek. The stockholders sent him back in May 1858 as the general agent of the Seneca Oil Company, with the fictitious title of "colonel" to lend him more prestige. His mission was to find a way to produce oil in quantity.

Drake spent several weeks digging in the main oil spring on the Hibbard farm. Unfortunately, he only struck water. Deciding to drill for oil, he traveled to Tarentum, near Pittsburgh, to observe the drilling of salt wells. He acquired a six-horsepower steam engine to power the drill, which was a cable tool that operated via percussion and not the modern rotary type (see chapter 7). Drake spent the winter of 1858 constructing a derrick to support the drill. He hired William A. "Uncle Billy" Smith, a blacksmith and experienced salt driller. Their first efforts were stymied by groundwater flooding, until they cased the well by driving a cast iron pipe down the hole with an oak battering ram. They resumed drilling in August 1859, by which time the company was nearly out of money and wanted to shut down the operation.

On August 27, 1859, work stopped after the drill slipped through a crevice at a depth of 69.5 feet. The next day, Uncle Billy noticed oil floating at the top of the well, confirming that they had made a discovery. Figure 4.2 depicts a generalized cross section, running perpendicular to Oil Creek, under the area of the first Drake well. It illustrates how fortuitous was Drake's choice of location. Drake encountered, at 69.5 feet deep, an oil-bearing sand of relatively limited extent, both in the plane of the cross section and in the direction perpendicular to it. If he had drilled elsewhere in the immediate area, he could easily have missed it. To encounter the main oil-producing sand in this area, the Venango Third Sand (see chapter 7), he would have had to drill initially to a depth of over 400 feet. Drake did drill a second, deeper well nearby, striking oil at 480 feet. The first well produced about twenty barrels per day, the second one about twenty-four, which were low rates of production by the standards that would soon be established.

A frantic oil boom followed Drake's discoveries, launching the modern US oil industry (see chapter 5). Drake left the oil industry in 1863. He had served for a time as president of the Seneca Oil Company but was not a good manager and had been forced to resign in 1860. Although he had paved the way for others to become wealthy, he made only a modest sum, and he eventually managed to lose that through poor investments. In 1873 his friends in Titusville convinced the Pennsylvania legislature to provide him with a pension,

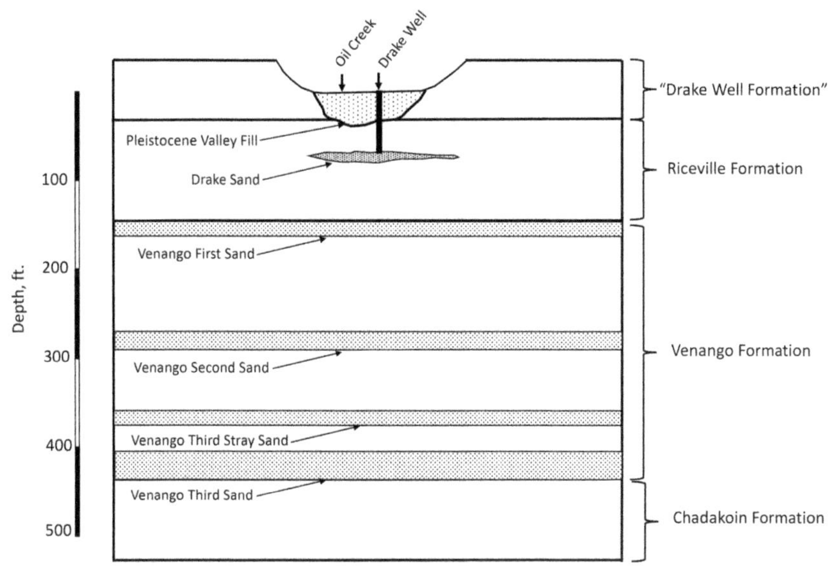

Figure 4.2. Generalized Sketch Cross Section, Running Perpendicular to Oil Creek, under the Area of the Drake Well. Drake was fortunate to encounter, at 69.5 feet deep, an oil-bearing sand of relatively limited extent, both in the plane of the cross section and in the direction perpendicular to it. *Source*: Adapted from a figure in Harper (1998).

in recognition of his contributions to the state's economy. Drake lived with debilitating muscular illness in Bethlehem, Pennsylvania, until his death on November 8, 1880.

As for the Seneca Oil Company, after several more management changes and continuing poor performance, it sold its Pennsylvania interests to George W. Steele of Brooklyn, New York, on March 7, 1864 for $10,000. The company that helped begin the modern oil industry in America then ceased operating. None of the New Haven investors made any money from the venture. James Townsend had paid in about $50,000 and gotten a similar amount back. Jonathan Eveleth, Bissell's partner, died in 1862. The New Haven investors ceased their involvement in the oil regions, but Bissell did not. He left his law practice in New York and moved to Franklin, Pennsylvania, where he remained until 1864. Along with a number of financial partners from New York, he invested heavily in oil lands around Franklin, on the McClintock Farm, and elsewhere. He was successful and also participated in many other commercial developments, including railroads. He died in New York City, a wealthy man, on November 18, 1884. Despite his success, he reportedly remained bitter toward Townsend and the rest of the New Haven group.

Table 4.1. Some Notable Early Oil Wells

Operator or director	*Date*	*Location*	*Was oil the explicit purpose?*	*Was there an associated oil company?*	*Was the well drilled?*	*Depth (feet)*	*Engine-powered?*	*Was the well cased?*	*Did the well spark an oil business boom?*	*References*
Kasimbey Mansurbekov	1803	Azerbaijan; Bibi-Eibat offshore	Yes	Unknown	No	Shallow	No	NA	No	Mir-Babayev (2021)
David and Joseph Ruffner	1806–1808	USA: Western Virginia, near Charleston	No	No	Yes	58	No	Rudimentary wooden tube lowered into hole	No	McKain and Allen (1994); Williamson and Daum (1959)
Robert McKee and Silas Thorla	1814, 1816	USA: Caldwell, Ohio	No	No	Yes	c. 200	No	Unknown	No	Camp (2016)
Martin Beatty, Marcus Huling, and Andrew Zimmerman	December 4, 1818	USA: Kentucky	No	No	Yes	170	No	Unknown	No	Nuttall (2014); Sorenson (2020)
Capt. G.W. Hunt	1820	USA: Kentucky	No	No	Yes	Unknown	No	Unknown	No	Nuttall (2014); Sorenson (2020)
Col. Emerson	March 11, 1829	USA: Kentucky	No	No	Yes	175	No	Unknown	No	Nuttall (2014); Sorenson (2020)
Various	1825 and before	Azerbaijan; Surakhani	Yes	Unknown	No	Up to 20	No	NA	No	Eichwald (1834); Mir-Babayev (2011)

Rathbone family	June 24, 1842	USA: Western Virginia	No	No	Yes	300	No	Unknown	No	McKain and Allen (1994)
Vasili Nikolayevich Semyonov; Major Alexeev	July 14, 1846	Azerbaijan: Bibi-Eibat, near Baku	Yes	No (auspices of Russian govern-ment)	Yes	69	No	No	No	Mir-Babayev (2008, 2011, 2017)
Andrés Pico	1850	USA: Pico Canyon, Los Angeles County, California	Yes	No	No	Near surface	No	NA	No	Prutzman (1913)
George Lemon	Early 1850s	USA: western Virginia	Possibly for both salt and oil	No	Yes	c. 50	No (water powered)	Unknown	No	McKain and Allen (1994)
Ignacy Łukasiewicz	1853	Austria-Hungary: Bóbrka, Galicia	Yes	Yes	No	Near surface	No	NA	Moderate	Sozanski et al. (2006); Frank (2005)
Theodor and Marin Mehedin-ţeanu (refiners using crude from preexisting and new pits)	1856–1857	Romania: Ploieşti area	Yes	Yes	No	Various	No	NA	No	Rovinaru et al. (2015); Rizea (2017); Dimancescu (2020)

(Continued)

Table 4.1. (Continued)

Operator or director	*Date*	*Location*	*Was oil the explicit purpose?*	*Was there an associated oil company?*	*Was the well drilled?*	*Depth (feet)*	*Engine-powered?*	*Was the well cased?*	*Did the well spark an oil business boom?*	*References*
James Miller Williams	August 26, 1858	Canada: Oil Springs, Ontario	Yes (Sought bitumen, found crude oil as well)	Yes	No	Reports vary from 10 to 49 feet	No	NA	No	Gray (2008a,b)
James Miller Williams	Possibly 1859	Canada: Oil Springs, Ontario	Yes	Yes	Yes	146	No	Unknown	No	Gray (2008a)
Lewis Ross	1859	USA: Oklahoma	No	No	Maybe	Near Surface	No	Unknown	No	Skelton (2006); Sorenson (2009)
Robert W. Hazlett	Early to mid-1859	USA: Oil Spring Run, near Petroleum, western Virginia	Yes	Yes	Yes	Unknown	Unknown	Unknown	No	McKain and Allen (1994)
Edwin L. Drake	August 27, 1859	USA: Near Oil Creek, Venango County, Pennsylvania	Yes	Yes	Yes	69.5	Yes	Yes	Yes	Brice (2009)

SO . . . WHO DRILLED THE FIRST MODERN, INDUSTRIAL OIL WELL?

The contest is really between the 1846 Baku well and the 1859 Drake well, and one's choice of winner depends on the weight one assigns to the various criteria outlined earlier. The 1846 Baku well has a very good claim on being the first modern industrial oil well. It was drilled, not hand dug, and done so deliberately to find oil. However, the Azerbaijani well fails according to some other relevant criteria. Unlike Drake's well, drilling was done manually using a percussion rod and was not powered by a steam engine. Also, the hole was probably not cased. Perhaps more importantly, there was no organized corporation backing the effort: it was entirely a venture of the Tsarist government. Unlike Drake's well, the Azerbaijani well did not result in any increased commercial activity or competition. In fact, the Tsarist government explicitly forbade the private exploration for oil. The modern industry in Azerbaijan would not begin to take off until almost three decades later, after 1872, when Tsar Alexander II opened oil exploration and development to the private sector (See chapter 6). Overall, there is thus also a good case for recognizing the Drake well as the first fully modern commercial, industrial oil well.

Chapter 5

Nineteenth-Century Oil in the United States

During the nineteenth century, the main oil-producing provinces were in the eastern part of the country. The Appalachian one was the earliest, including portions of the states of Pennsylvania, Virginia (now West Virginia), and Ohio, with some activity in Kentucky and New York as well. Another major area well established before 1900 was the Lima-Indiana giant field complex of Ohio and Indiana. As indicated in the sketch map of figure 5.1, the Mid-Continent Oil Region—including parts of Oklahoma, Kansas, and Texas—was still an emerging province in the nineteenth century. The first discoveries were made, but major production did not take place until after 1900. The same was true of California.

The story of the modern oil industry in the United States, following Drake's 1859 well, began as one of nearly untrammeled free enterprise and competition. This was enabled in part by the unique legal situation in the United States, in which landowners generally own not just the surface land, but the resources beneath it as well. In other countries, subsurface resources have generally belonged to the state or the crown. In the United States, subsurface rights are also severable from surface ownership; they can be sold separately or leased. Prospectors explored for and developed oil on their own land, or they leased the right to do so from someone else, generally in exchange for a payment that could take the form of a portion of the oil produced. In the early 1860s in Pennsylvania, this was generally between a quarter and a third (Williamson and Daum 1959). It should be noted that mineral rights in the United States can also be owned by the federal, state, local, and tribal governments—though nineteenth-century development was focused on states with low levels of public mineral ownership.

The evolution of subsurface rights was more complicated in states such as California and Texas that had formerly belonged to the Spanish Crown.

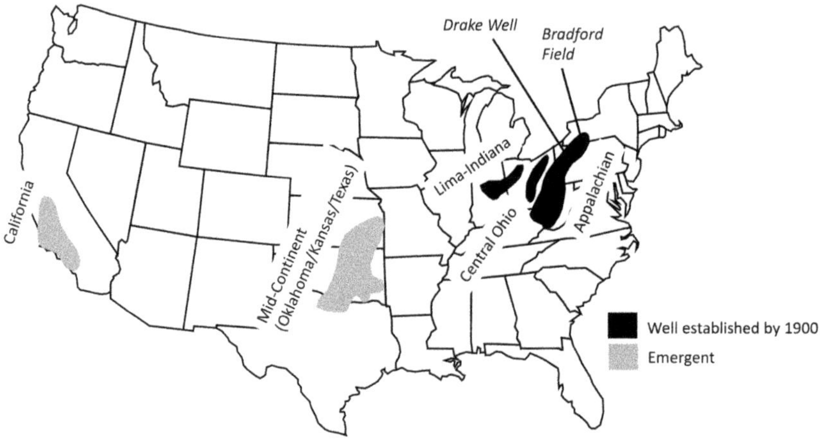

Figure 5.1. Generalized Sketch Map Showing Rough Extent and Location of Oil-Producing Regions of the United States during the Nineteenth Century. The Appalachian, Ohio, and Indiana regions were well established by 1900. California and the Mid-Continent region were opened up in the nineteenth century but did not become major producers until the twentieth. *Source*: Drawn using some information on a map in Day (1922, 76–77).

When those territories belonged to Spain, the crown had rights to subsurface resources, not the landowners. When the territories passed to Mexico, the resources passed to the Mexican government. After Texas became an independent republic in 1836, it initially followed Mexican law with respect to subsurface resources but moved to English common law in 1840. A series of disputes over rights to subsurface salt eventually clarified the doctrine that landowners owned rights to subsurface resources (Gruy 2000, 1–2).

In California, courts ruling on disputes between miners and landowners in the years after the gold rush of 1848 upheld the Mexican principle of state ownership of subsurface rights, effectively ruling in favor of miners. The California legislature in 1860 passed the Possessory Act, allowing agricultural settlers to claim 160 acres of public land as long as no mines or minerals were present. An amendment also allowed miners to prospect on land owned by others for agriculture or grazing. Prominent landowners, including the Fremont family, fought against these laws and rulings and were eventually able to get them invalidated by the US Supreme Court in 1858 (Gruy 2000, 2). In California, too, subsurface rights would belong to landowners.

The oil industry in the nineteenth-century United States thus began developing entirely through private enterprise, with myriad transactions between private parties. The federal government, and state governments, generally did not control or interfere in operations or competition. Restraints to competition came later in the century, largely from the growth of Standard Oil and its adoption of monopolistic practices. When the federal government did intervene, it was to rein in Standard Oil and restore a more competitive environment, as we discuss in the following sections.

PENNSYLVANIA

The story of the Drake well of 1859 is told in chapter 4. In the following sections, we discuss developments before and after Drake.

Before Drake

Samuel Kier

In the 1840s, merchant Samuel Kier began to notice the oil that flowed as an undesirable by-product from his father's brine wells in Tarentum, Pennsylvania. In 1848 he began bottling it and marketing it as a patent medicine. He advertised it as "Kier's Petroleum or Rock Oil, nature's remedy celebrated for its wonderful curative powers, taken from a well in Allegheny, Pa., four hundred feet below the earth's surface" (Derrick 1898, 11). The oil was claimed to ameliorate suffering due to rheumatism, gout, neuralgia, colds, sores, and a host of other problems, including diabetes. Kier also called the petroleum "Seneca Oil," after the local Native Americans who had reportedly long used the substance for medicinal purposes. The sales of patent medicine produced reasonable revenue but did not consume all the oil flowing out of the wells.

Kier sought other uses for the oil and in 1850 began experimenting with it as an illuminant. Crude oil produced too much smoke and an unpleasant odor. He sought help from Professor Booth, a Philadelphia chemist, who advised him to distill the oil. By doing so, he was eventually able to produce a fairly effective illuminant, probably similar to kerosene, that he marketed as "carbon oil." He built a single-barrel still on Seventh Avenue in Pittsburgh, becoming one of America's first oil refiners. Kier's business records show that he was selling his "carbon oil" as early as 1851. By 1853 Kier's product was selling for $1.50 a gallon ($63 per barrel, an enormous sum at the time). Brice (2008) provides an excellent account of Kier's life and work.

The Drake Aftermath

After Drake's well, there was an almost immediate rush to obtain leases in the vicinity, in the valley of Oil Creek, Venango County. There were forty-three

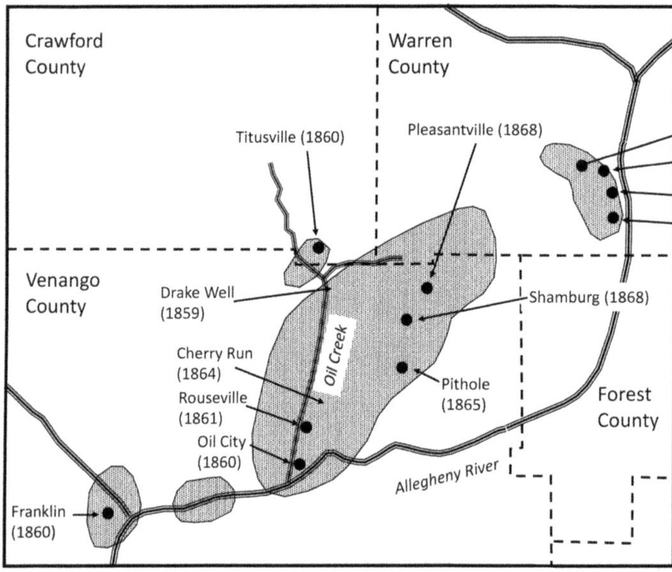

Figure 5.2. Generalized Sketch Map of the Earliest Oil-Producing Regions of Northwestern Pennsylvania in the 1860s. Areas with a relatively high density of oil production are indicated by shading. Although such areas are depicted as continuous, this does not imply one large, continuous oil field; the map is a simplification. Numbers in parentheses indicate the year of oil discovery near a particular location. Dashed lines indicate county boundaries. Some early oil regions lie outside the area of the map, including those of Butler and Armstrong Counties to the south. *Source*: Adapted and generalized from a map in Williamson and Daum (1959), with additional information. Dates are from Derrick (1898).

farms in the narrow valley, which is roughly sixteen miles long between Titusville and the point where Oil Creek flows into the Allegheny River. The valley is flanked by steep hillsides. Jonathan Watson, of the lumber firm Brewer, Watson, from which Drake had leased mineral rights, rode all over the valley on horseback to obtain leases of his own in the days after Drake's strike. He would become a leading producer in the area, drilling 2,000 wells by 1871 (Williamson and Daum 1959, 87). George Bissell, too, bought or leased land in the valley with his partner J.G. Eveleth. Bissell also shrewdly built a factory in the town of Franklin to manufacture barrels for oil storage and transport. Bissell amassed a large fortune quickly and left the area in 1863, although he remained involved in the business and established a bank at Petroleum Center in 1866 servicing the industry. Watson and Bissell were soon followed by hundreds of others seeking fortunes in the early oil region.

One well drilled by Brewer, Watson, in the early years deserves some attention not because of the volume of its production, but because of its longevity. McClintock No. 1 was drilled using human leg power to kick the drill down. The well struck oil in August 1861, at a depth of 620 feet, initially producing 175 barrels a day. It continued producing for 150 years. Today the well is owned by the Pennsylvania Historical and Museum Commission and is pumped quarterly to produce oil earning just enough income to maintain the site (Drake Well 2021).

Expansion on Oil Creek

As shown in figure 5.2, by the end of 1860, exploration and development had extended down Oil Creek to Rouseville and almost as far south as Oil City, on the McClintock Farm, as well as north to Titusville. Activity also extended northeast beyond the valley to Tidioute in Warren County and west to Franklin. By June 1860 there were twenty-one wells along Oil Creek, six at Tidioute, and five at Franklin, producing a combined total of 200 barrels per day. By November 1860 there were seventy-four wells in Venango County producing nearly 1,200 barrels per day. In the next year, Venango County produced an average of roughly 5,500 barrels per day (Williamson and Daum 1959, 102–103). Even so, refiners were slow to switch from coal oil to petroleum for kerosene production, as the true extent of petroleum resources was unknown.

Early Gushers

Some of this uncertainty began to be resolved after Pennsylvania's first gusher, struck on April 17, 1861. Henry Rouse drilled deeper in an existing well near the mouth of Oil Creek, extending it from the 150-foot depth from which it was modestly producing at the time, to 300 feet. Oil began spewing out to a height of 60 feet above the surface, at a rate of roughly 3,000 barrels per day. Rouse and eighteen others died trying vainly to control the well as natural gas ignited and exploded when it hit a hot boiler in a neighboring area. The fire burned for three days.

Rouse's gusher was followed the next month by the Fountain well on the McElhenny Farm, which found oil at a depth of 460 feet about seven miles north along Oil Creek. This was the first well known to have been drilled purposely to strike the "Third Sand" (see chapter 7). The Empire well was struck on the same farm, from the Third Sand, in September 1861, flowing at 2,500 barrels a day for eight months, but declining thereafter. Despite the decline of the Empire well, several other gushers kept the McElhenny Farm producing up to 6,000 barrels a day through mid-1863. Meanwhile, a number of other properties joined the McElhenny Farm as leading producers, including the Tarr, McClintock, Buchanan, and Blood Farms. Phillips No. 2, on the Tarr

Farm, was struck in October 1861, flowing initially at up to 4,000 barrels a day. It was soon joined before the end of the year by other prolific Tarr wells, Woodward and Elephant No. 2.

The effects of the early gushers were manifold. On the one hand, they increased confidence that large quantities of petroleum were indeed discoverable and encouraged further exploration and development. On the other hand, they caused oversupply and a dramatic collapse in prices, from two dollars per barrel during summer 1861 to ten cents a barrel by the end of the year (note this is not reflected in the prices shown in table D.6, which only provides annual averages). The gushers also dramatically illustrated the mismatch between production capacity and the ability to store and transport oil.

Beyond Oil Creek

Cherry Run

Until 1864, oil production in Pennsylvania was dominated by the Oil Creek Valley in Venango County. As shown in figure 5.2, this changed as production began at Cherry Run, a tributary of Oil Creek. William Reed struck oil on July 28, 1864, with a well flowing 300 barrels a day. Within a month, all the land near Cherry Run was bought up or leased, there were 300 drilling operations, and production reached 1,000 barrels a day.

Pithole

In 1865 the Pithole Creek district was opened up. Pithole Creek roughly paralleled Oil Creek to the east, and like Oil Creek, flowed into the Allegheny. On January 7, I.G. Frazier of the United States Oil Company completed a well, producing initially at 650 barrels a day from a depth of 600 feet, on the Holmden Farm (Carll 1890, 29). The Kilgore and Keenan wells, drilled on the same farm about two weeks later, produced initially at 800 barrels per day.

This led to the rapid construction of the new city of Pithole, attracting large numbers of explorers and speculators. By June 1865 Pithole had four gushers producing more than 2,000 barrels per day, and these were followed by several others. Three thousand teamsters arrived in Pithole that month, and by July the new post office was processing 5,000 letters a day, making Pithole the third-busiest city in Pennsylvania in postal terms, after Philadelphia and Pittsburgh. The population swelled to 15,000 by September.

Crime and vice were rife, leading one journalist to dub Pithole "the sewer city" (Williamson and Daum 1959, 123). Pithole sparked a national speculative frenzy in oil company stocks, most of which proved worthless. The city declined almost as rapidly as it grew up. The very high spatial density of wells led to serious drops in gas pressure so that oil production declined from over 6,000 barrels per day in 1865 to around 200 in 1870 (Carll 1890, 29). The population began emptying out in 1866 and was near zero in 1868. Today Pithole is a ghost town.

Benehoff and Pioneer Runs

The rapid decline of output in Pithole was offset by the development of two new producing areas in Venango and Warren Counties. The first was at Benehoff Run, a small stream flowing into Oil Creek. There the Ocean Oil Company of Philadelphia struck a gusher at a depth of 600 feet, flowing 300 barrels per day. Situated at an elevation of 170 feet, the well was the first success on high ground, as opposed to low-lying areas adjacent to streams. By 1866 there were 150 wells being drilled or producing near Benehoff Run, with a total flow of 2,100 barrels per day. This was soon augmented with production from nearby Pioneer Run, initiated by the Lady Brooks gusher of April 1866. The nearby hamlet of Petroleum Center quickly mushroomed to a population of 3,000 and began echoing Pithole in lawlessness.

The second new area of 1866 and 1867 was in Warren County, near Tidioute, along tributaries of the Allegheny River. Particularly important were the areas of West Hickory Creek and Dennis Run, the latter having been first opened up in late 1865. The oil at West Hickory Creek was struck at relatively shallow depths of 200–300 feet and was of a quality that made it useful for lubrication. Wells in Dennis Run were too closely spaced, as they had been at Pithole, causing degradation. The same happened at nearby Triumph Hill, close to Tidioute, where strikes on high ground initially helped offset some of Dennis Run's decline. The Warren County producing area would experience another renaissance in 1870 with the opening of the Fagundas field.

Later Districts

The year 1868 brought new producing districts in Shamburg and Pleasantville, north of Pithole. In the Shamburg area, every well drilled that year struck oil. Nearby Pleasantville, opened up by Abram James with his Harmonial No. 1 Well, quickly became a speculative boomtown along the lines of Pithole. Once again, overcrowding of wells hastened decline.

An important set of new developments in the early 1870s was in the new "Lower Oil Region" of Clarion, Butler, and Armstrong Counties, whose production would equal that of the Oil Creek area in 1872 and then greatly exceed it in the ensuing decade (see figure 5.3). Further discussion of the expanding Pennsylvania oil industry in the 1860s can be found in Williamson and Daum (1959); Adomites and Bernik (2010); Henry (1873); Derrick (1898).

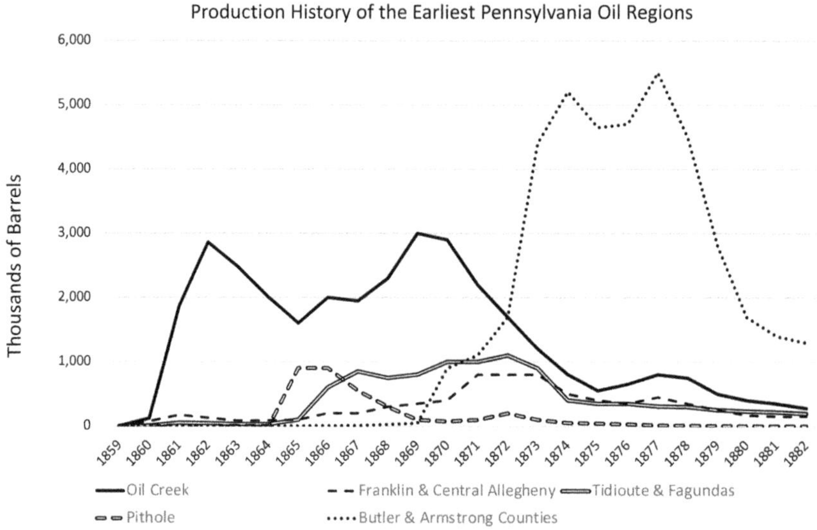

Figure 5.3. Oil Production History of the Earliest Pennsylvania Oil Regions, 1859–1882, Showing the Short-Lived Dominance of the Original Region around Oil Creek. Oil Creek includes Cherry Run, Rouseville, Pleasantville, and Shamburg. *Source*: From data in Carll (1890, 29).

Bradford

All the early Pennsylvania Oil Regions were eventually eclipsed by the transformative discovery of the giant Bradford field in 1871. The Bradford field was the most prolific and also the last of the major fields discovered in Pennsylvania. The northernmost field in the Pennsylvania oil region, it lies mainly in the north central part of McKean County and extends into Cattaraugus County in the state of New York. Figure 5.4 shows the rapid swamping of all the other regions by Bradford by the end of the 1870s.

Bradford's discovery was a complex affair, occurring in fits and starts, as discussed by Harper (2013). Early drilling attempts in the area, beginning in 1861, came up dry or found very small quantities of oil. Daniel Kingsbury drilled a well in 1865 or 1866 and struck some oil at 791 feet. The oil had good lubricating properties and was sold as such for a few years. In 1865 an entrepreneur named Job Moses deepened a preexisting 1,000-foot deep well in Limestone, New York, by 50 feet, and struck commercial quantities of oil. This is not generally considered the Bradford discovery well, but it pointed the way. The actual November 1871 discovery well was also drilled by Moses, along with J.E. Butts and C.H. Foster. After forming the Foster Oil Company, they struck oil just north of the city of Bradford, Pennsylvania, at

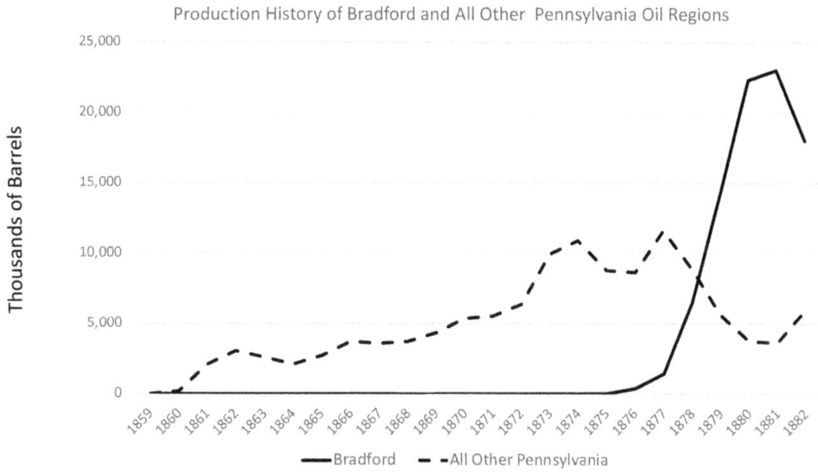

Figure 5.4. Oil Production History of the Bradford Region, Compared with All Other Pennsylvania Oil Regions Combined, 1859–1882. ***Source*****: From data in Carll (1890, 29).**

a depth of 1,100 feet. The well flowed a modest ten barrels of oil per day, but it had tapped the main reservoir of the Bradford Oil Field, the Bradford Third Sand. The formation was so named because drillers and operators thought it was the same "Third Sand" that produced in Venango County (see chapter 7 for a brief discussion of the sands). As it turned out, the two formations did not correlate, but the name stuck. Interest in Bradford increased three years later when Butts and Foster drilled a well just northeast of the city that initially flowed 70 barrels per day, soon rising to 200. Activity increased, and by 1880 7,500 wells had been drilled (Harper 2013, 24).

A complete production history of Bradford to 1900 is given in table D.5. It is not an exceptionally large field by the standards set in the twentieth century but was a major find by the standards of its time. It reached a peak production of 22.945 million barrels in 1881. As shown in figure 1.6 (chapter 1), Bradford produced about 11 percent of the world's oil in the nineteenth century overall, but in the three years of 1880, 1881, and 1882, it produced 74 percent of all the oil produced in the United States and 64 percent of all the oil produced in the world. No other oil field since then has dominated global production to such an extent. As Bradford production increased, prices dropped, from $2.56 a barrel in 1876 to $1.19 in 1878 (see table D.6).

Bradford production declined steeply from 1881 to 1887, when it was about 4.5 million barrels. After that, production declined more gradually.

Many wells had been abandoned, and a number were not properly plugged, so that freshwater accidentally entered. In some cases, this flooding led to improved production in nearby wells, and the industry began using intentional waterflooding to increase production. The practice was illegal in Pennsylvania but would eventually be legalized in 1921.

The Bradford experience would lead to the later development of scientific waterflooding methods to enhance production—a new secondary oil-recovery mechanism. Waterflooding would lead in the early twentieth century to a renaissance in Bradford production, which would reach 16.739 million barrels in 1937—almost the 1882 level. Thereafter, production would decline again.

WESTERN VIRGINIA AND WEST VIRGINIA

As we have observed in chapter 4, there was considerable pre-Drake activity in western Virginia, including a well that may have been contemporaneous with Drake's in 1859, though less famous. Drake's discovery stimulated increased activity in western Virginia. In 1860 Samuel D. Karns drilled a well along the Kanawha River near Elizabeth, Wirt County, that produced 37–50 barrels per day. This was in the Burning Springs, or Kanawha, District. Another well toward the end of the year produced 200–250 barrels per day of light oil suitable for processing into kerosene, encouraging prospectors. By spring 1861, production was up to 800 barrels per day (Williamson and Daum 1859, 102). A town quickly sprang up in Burning Springs, and it was lit by natural gas.

The US Civil War that began in 1861 put a damper on Virginia oil production, and indeed in 1863 Burning Springs was raided by the Confederate Army, as we discuss in a separate section. However, activity did not completely cease, and the Volcano field, also known as the White Oak field, was discovered in 1863, near the quickly developed boomtown (and current ghost town) of Volcano in the western part of the soon-to-be state of West Virginia. Another important field, Horseneck, was also discovered in 1863, with a gusher well. There was drilling and development after the Civil War, and refineries sprang up in Parkersburg, which became an oil hub not only for West Virginia but also for neighboring southeastern Ohio. However, production levels in West Virginia remained insignificant compared to the juggernaut that was Pennsylvania during this time period. As late as 1890, West Virginia production was only 1.7 percent that of Pennsylvania. However, it rose thirty-three-fold over the next decade and in 1900 exceeded the declining production of Pennsylvania. This was largely due to the 1888 discovery of the prolific Mannington field—perhaps the first major field discovered with the explicit aid of petroleum geology and the anticlinal theory, as discussed in chapter 7.

Oil and the Birth of a New State

West Virginia was created from fifty northwestern counties of the Commonwealth of Virginia during the US Civil War of 1861–1865. Effectively, it amounted to a secession from a secession: Virginia seceded from the Union and joined the Confederacy on May 23, 1861; West Virginia seceded from Virginia and rejoined the Union as the thirty-fifth state on June 20, 1863. After becoming a state, it formed five more counties within its borders. The two easternmost counties of Berkeley and Jefferson, part of the original fifty, refused to recognize inclusion but were compelled to do so by the US Congress in 1866.

The formation of West Virginia was a complicated process, succinctly summarized by Williams (2021). A highly simplified sequence of the events is as follows. There were three conventions held in the city of Wheeling during 1861. In the second of these, held in June, Virginia's northwestern counties created a shadow state of Virginia that still belonged to the Union, with a shadow government called the "Restored Government of Virginia," to pave the way for creation and admission of the new state. On August 20, 1861, the Restored Government passed a bill for the creation of a new state; the bill was ratified by public referendum on October 24. Turnout was low in the referendum, not least because so many men were absent, fighting for the Confederacy. President Lincoln dismissed the low turnout, saying that it was customary "to give no legal consideration whatever to those who do not choose to vote" (Williams 2021). The third convention met in November to create a constitution for the new state. The federal cabinet was divided on whether to admit the new state or not, but on December 31, 1862, President Lincoln issued his approval.

West Virginia's secession involved a number of issues that predated the Civil War. There was tension between the growing industrial interests—including oil interests—of the northwestern part of Virginia and the plantation-dominated remainder of the state, where the institution of slavery was also more firmly entrenched. The planters controlled the government in Richmond, and the industrial interests felt underrepresented. Thus, it is no surprise that oilmen and oil money played a prominent role in the Wheeling conventions. The oil interests also had a very strong ally in the Baltimore and Ohio Railroad, whose president John W. Garrett also happened to be a friend of both Abraham Lincoln and secretary of war Edwin Stanton.

Oilmen and oil investors who were involved in the statehood conventions included John Jay Jackson Sr., John Jay Jackson Jr., Thomas S. Conley, J.C. Rathbone, Jacob Beeson Blair, P.G. Van Winkle, John Moss, G.W. Henderson, and A. Mather, among many others (McKain and Allen 1994, 51). In fact,

John Moss, an early investor in Burning Springs, was elected president of the First Wheeling Convention. It would be a gross exaggeration to assert that West Virginia split from Virginia because of oil. However, oil industrialists and their money, joined with other interests, helped tilt a delicate balance of power in favor of secession from Virginia and statehood. One very powerful person in northwestern Virginia was J.B. Ford, superintendent of the Wheeling division of the Baltimore & Ohio Railroad; he controlled wartime use of the railroad. He also happened to be a co-owner of an important oil field at Petroleum. In addition to protecting the railroad, he had an incentive to protect his oil field. Newly wealthy oil industrialists did not want to see that wealth co-opted by Virginia planters and the Confederacy, and when their desires linked with railroad interests and abolitionist forces, they were powerful enough to make statehood happen.

An illustration of oil influence can be found in one of the first acts of the new state's legislature in February 1863—before official statehood. The act created the Rathbone Petroleum Company and was a direct intervention in favor of oil interests. The Rathbone family were major leaseholders in Burning Springs, and W.P. Rathbone's death in 1862 resulted in all the leases, as well as other transactions, being tied up in his estate and subject to lengthy court proceedings. The act settled the partition at a stroke, "so that the public will not be deprived of this valuable production" (McKain and Allen 1994, 55). And perhaps no better evidence for the influence of oil in West Virginia's creation can be found than by simply looking at the state seal: oil barrels on the obverse and an oil derrick on the reverse (see figure 5.5).

Figure 5.5. The Seal of the State of West Virginia, Depicting Oil Barrels on the Obverse (Left) and an Oil Derrick on the Reverse (Right). ***Source*****: Public domain images (https://sos.wv.gov/admin-law/Pages/WVSeal.aspx), originally in color but rendered here in monochrome.**

The First Wartime Raid on an Oil Field

On May 9, 1863, while the Civil War was raging, a Confederate Army unit led by General William E. "Grumble" Jones conducted a raid on Burning Springs. While it is not certain that the oilfield was the intended target, the preponderance of evidence suggests that it was. Union intelligence reported that an oilfield somewhere was to be attacked. Rumors of these reports reached the Pennsylvania oil fields as well, and some of them went on alert and reduced operations. However, the Confederates did not head for Pennsylvania, but rather for Burning Springs. There were actually Union troops in the area near the oil fields, but the Union command moved them away, deeming it more important to protect the city of Parkersburg and the B&O Railroad. While the oil fields were recognized as economically important, and generated about a dollar a barrel in taxes for the Union, the railroad was critical for troop transport and the conduct of the war.

The Confederate raiders set fire to the oil field over a period of nine hours, destroying eighty to one hundred wells, all the equipment and infrastructure, and all oil stored for shipping. As General Jones wrote to Robert E. Lee, commander of the Army of Northern Virginia:

> [W]e marched on Oiltown (Burning Springs or Rathbone City), where we arrived May 9. The wells were owned mainly by Southern men, now driven from their homes and their property appropriated, either by the Federal Government or Northern men. This oil is used extensively as a lubricator of machinery and for illumination. All the oil, the tanks, barrels, engines for pumping, engine houses and wagons, in a word, everything used in raising, holding, or sending it off was burned. The boats, filled with oil in bulk, burst with a report almost equaling artillery, and spread the burning fluid over the river. Before night high columns of ebony smoke marked the meanderings of the stream as far as the eye could reach. By dusk the oil from the tanks on the burning creek had reached the river, and the whole stream became a sheet of fire. A burning stream carrying destruction to our merciless enemy, was a scene of magnificence that might well carry joy to every patriotic heart. Men of experience estimated the oil destroyed at 150,000 barrels. It will be many months before a large supply can be had from this source, as it can only be boated down the Little Kanawha when the water is high (McKain and Allen 1994, 41).

Jones's figure of 150,000 destroyed barrels of oil was almost certainly a gross exaggeration. The field produced less than half that every year. Charles H. Shattuck, an important West Virginia oilman, estimated the destruction at 20,000 barrels. The destruction was not permanent, and operators began rebuilding soon after the raid.

OHIO

Ohio is of considerable importance to the history of oil, not least because Standard Oil was founded and headquartered there, as we discuss in a separate section later. The development of oil in Ohio can be roughly divided into two broad regions: eastern Ohio, which is essentially part of the broad historical Appalachian oil province that includes western Pennsylvania and West Virginia, and northwestern Ohio, where the giant Lima-Indiana field was discovered.

Eastern Ohio

Aside from the early oil finds while drilling for salt, mentioned in chapter 4, the first truly commercial oil well in Ohio was at Macksburg in 1860. It was manually drilled using a hand lever and found oil at a depth of 59 feet (Camp 2016). The oil was viscous and not the best for producing kerosene, but it had good lubricating properties and was sold for that purpose. It was initially shipped along the Muskingum River to the nearby city of Marietta, which is on the Ohio River. From there it could be taken to Pittsburgh by boat with relative ease. The Civil War interrupted the industry in the Macksburg area, but in 1874 a gusher drilled by George Rice renewed interest. In the 1880s deeper drilling (1,400–1,900 feet) to the Berea Sandstone was successful. A peak in monthly production of nearly 80,000 barrels was reached in July 1885, followed by decline; the area was of relatively minor importance after 1890.

In 1861 a group of investors led by John Newton drilled near a stream called Cow Run, also not far from Marietta. Interest had been sparked partly by the presence of gas bubbles in the stream. The group struck oil at a depth of 137 feet, producing initially at fifty barrels per day. Oil was at first transported by wagon to Marietta, then by boat to Saint Louis, via the Ohio and Mississippi rivers. In 1868 a 5.5-mile pipeline was built to the Ohio River, but by the 1870s the Cow Run Field was all but exhausted. Elsewhere in southeastern Ohio, drillers from the Titusville area in Pennsylvania spread into Morgan County. In 1860 a well found a modest amount of at a depth of 65 feet. Further drilling brought more success, and by the 1890s the oil-producing area was known as the Chesterhill Oil Field.

There were many other nineteenth-century discoveries in eastern Ohio, including a considerable amount of gas in the central and northern part of the region. Camp (2016) provides a good account.

Northwestern Ohio: The Lima-Indiana Field

The Lima-Indiana field, also called the Trenton field after its prolific reservoir rock, the Trenton Limestone, is located in northwestern Ohio and Indiana. It covers a large area that extends, with interruptions, from Lake Erie to Marion,

Indiana. The field produced 514 million barrels of oil over its lifetime. The field made Ohio the top oil-producing state in the United States from 1895, when it surpassed Pennsylvania, to 1902, when it was surpassed in turn by California. The Ohio portion of the Lima-Indiana field peaked in 1897, and the smaller Indiana portion peaked in 1906. The field as a whole produced 68,500 barrels per day in 1896, amounting to 41.1 percent of the oil output of the United States. By 1910 85 percent of its recoverable 514 million barrels had already been extracted. In 1914 its production was 13,700 barrels per day, or 1.9 percent of US output (which had grown greatly from other fields).

The first hydrocarbon discovery in the Trenton Limestone was in the form of natural gas. Gas seeps were long known in the area of Findlay, Ohio, and gas may have been used there as early as 1838. In 1884 a medical doctor, Charles Oesterlin, formed the Findlay Natural Gas Company and began drilling on his farm. In December 1884 Oesterlin struck gas at 1,092 feet. Several wells later, his company's January 20, 1886, Karg well flowed at up to 50 million cubic feet of gas a day from a depth of 1,146 feet (Spencer 2008, 59).

The first oil discovery in the field was by Benjamin Faurot, near Lima, Allen County, on May 19, 1885. The well struck at 1,251 feet, with an initial flow of 200 barrels per day (Spencer 2008, 62). Faurot and others formed the Trenton Rock Oil Company in 1886 and quickly drilled 250 wells in Lima and southwest into Indiana. Further north, near Findlay, the Fulton well of 1886 struck oil. September 1887 saw three gushers drilled in the Findlay area: Ducat, Potter, and Foltz, each flowing more than 1,000 barrels per day (Spencer 2008, 62). On the Indiana side, gas was discovered in 1885, and oil was discovered in 1889.

Lima-Indiana oil was sour—that is, high in sulfur. This made it difficult to use in lamps, as its products emitted a foul smell when burned. Nevertheless, it came to represent a competitive advantage for Standard Oil (see separate section). Standard, which had hitherto concentrated on downstream operations and shunned oil exploration and development, bought large amounts of Lima-Indiana producing property in the 1880s at attractive prices. Standard's head, John D. Rockefeller, had consulted with Herman Frasch, who developed a process to reduce the sulfur content of the oil. The company completed a large refinery at Whiting, Indiana, near Chicago, in 1890 for refining Lima crude via the Frasch process, and it soon converted other refineries. Standard could now use cheap Lima crude to produce refined products equal in quality to those from more expensive oil.

CALIFORNIA

The 1850s

As discussed in chapter 4, in the 1850s Andrés Pico collected crude oil from seeps found in the Pico Canyon in present-day Los Angeles County and distilled it to create illuminating oil for the San Fernando Mission. There were other early refining operations in the 1850s, although records are spotty. For example, Charles Morrell of San Francisco had such an operation producing kerosene in eastern Santa Barbara County in 1857 (Hanks 1884). In the same year, George S. Gilbert had a commercial refinery in southern California that may have been operating as early as 1857 (Testa 2001), producing roughly seven to ten barrels a week.

The 1860s—Early Drilled Wells

California's first large-scale oil activity was in the 1860s. The first well intentionally drilled for oil was in 1861, on the Davis Ranch in Humboldt County, northern California (Testa 2001). Later, in 1865, the Union well in the same area initially yielded about thirty barrels from a depth of about ninety feet, but did not prove a consistent producer and was abandoned. The optimistically named "Petrolia" oil field saw some development over the next century but never became a success (Aalto 2013).

Southern California would prove more prolific in the long run, although not in the 1860s. In 1864 Professor Benjamin Silliman Jr. of Yale University—the same man who had analyzed the oil of the Pennsylvania Rock Oil Company in 1855—arrived in present-day Ventura County. His purpose was to assess California's petroleum potential for eastern interests, including those of Thomas Scott, future head of the Pennsylvania Railroad. The refiner George Gilbert showed Silliman seeps along San Antonio Creek and on Sulphur Mountain. In his reports Silliman (1864, 1865) confidently proclaimed that California would yield large quantities of oil. As he put it, "The discovery of petroleum on a great scale in California is a fact now well established, and chiefly along or near the sea-shore, in the counties of San Luis Obispo, Santa Barbara and Los Angeles" (Silliman 1865, 3). Silliman's statements contributed to a speculative oil bubble in southern California in 1865. A number of companies failed, and Silliman's reputation suffered considerable damage. The irony is that southern California did eventually prove to have enormous quantities of oil, and Silliman would ultimately be proved correct.

The most successful well during this time period was drilled by Thomas R. Bard, nephew of Thomas Scott and future president of the Union Oil Company of California, in 1867, at Rancho Ojai near Ventura. He drilled with a steam-powered cable rig. The well, Ojai 6, was 550 feet deep and produced about fifteen to twenty barrels per day; it was Bard's sixth attempt, after five dry holes (Henderson 2001). In 1866, around the time Bard was drilling his dry holes, Josiah Stanford, brother of Leland Stanford (future founder of Stanford University), took a different approach: he tunneled upward into Sulphur Mountain, allowing oil from a reservoir to flow down the tunnels for collection. He produced twenty barrels per day (Henderson 2001). Stanford's tunneling approach was later adopted by Union Oil, which dug fifty tunnels into Sulphur Mountain in the 1890s. Some of Stanford's tunnels continued flowing oil for another century (Henderson 2001).

The 1870s and Beyond

Pico Canyon and the Beginnings of Chevron

In the 1870s, a more stable industry began to take hold in California. In 1876 Charles Alexander Mentry of the California Star Oil Works Company drilled Pico Canyon Well No. 4, which turned out to be the discovery well of the Newhall field. It was 370 feet deep, extended to 560 feet in 1877. It flowed initially at twenty-five barrels per day of high-quality light oil and is usually cited as California's first true commercial well (Owen 1975, 135; USDI 1957).

This early activity in Pico Canyon formed the seed for what was to become the Standard Oil Company of California, later Chevron. On September 10, 1879, Charles N. Felton, Lloyd Tevis, George Loomis, and others organized the Pacific Coast Oil Company, which acquired the assets of California Star Oil Works. By 1900 Pacific Coast had several producing wells in the Newhall field, a refinery near San Francisco, its own railroad tank cars, and a tanker named for George Loomis, its first president. In that year it was acquired by Standard Oil for $761,000 and would eventually become the Standard Oil Company of California, later Chevron. Pico Canyon Well No. 4 would go on to produce oil until 1990, when Chevron finally plugged it (Henderson 2001).

The Beginnings of Union Oil

The Union Oil Company of California was founded in 1890 by Lyman Stewart, Wallace Hardison, and Thomas R. Bard as the "union" of three oil companies in southern California unaffiliated with Standard Oil: Sespe Oil Company, Hardison and Stewart Oil Company, and Mission Transfer Company. This consolidated an already existing set of alliances. In the year of its founding, Union produced about 84,000 barrels—approximately a quarter of California's output (Welty and Taylor 1966).

Like the future Chevron Corporation, Hardison and Stewart Oil Company—and hence, Union Oil—had roots in Pico Canyon. After seven dry holes in Pico Canyon in southern California and almost out of money, the company struck a small amount of oil in 1884. They sold their interest to Pacific Coast Oil Company, the future Chevron. In 1885, Hardison and Stewart began commercial development in Adams Canyon in Ventura County, to the west of Los Angeles. Hardison and Stewart allied themselves with Thomas Bard, whose company Mission Transfer owned large tracts of land in Ventura County and also a refinery, storage tanks, and pipelines. Hardison and Stewart bought a half interest in Mission Transfer. The third Union component was the Sespe Oil Company, formed to drill in the Sespe Canyon. Bard was president, while Stewart and Hardison were majority owners. By 1886 Union's predecessor companies were producing about a tenth of California's output.

Union discovered new oil in Torrey Canyon and in 1892 purchased the Los Angeles Oil Company. That company had no oil but held promising land in southern California. Union began drilling immediately and brought in California's first major gusher, Adams No. 28. The well flowed 40,000 barrels before it was brought under control. Union did not have enough infrastructure to capture the oil. The great majority flowed down the Santa Clara River into the Pacific Ocean.

Union Oil was first headquartered in Santa Paula, California, in a building that now houses a petroleum museum. Thomas Bard was the company's first president. In 1894 Stewart replaced Bard as president. The two had disputed constantly since the company's formation. Stewart viewed Bard as a short-term profit taker, and Bard viewed Stewart as a poor manager. Bard continued to challenge Stewart for control of the company through the 1890s. In 1899 he attempted a hostile takeover but failed. A year later, he sold his shares and entered politics. He was elected in 1900 to complete an unexpired term in the US Senate. In 1900 Union Oil moved its headquarters to Los Angeles. That same year it created the first-known oil company geological research department, under petroleum geologist William Orcutt. Union would remain an important independent force in the oil industry until its acquisition by Chevron in 2005.

Edward Doheny and the Los Angeles City Field

After several years in Mexico and the southwestern United States, Edward Laurence Doheny arrived in Los Angeles in 1892. Seeing a man hauling tar in a wagon one day, Doheny asked what it was, and the man said it was "breer" (from Spanish *brea* for "pitch"). This supposedly convinced Doheny to prospect for oil. He had almost no financial resources but persuaded his friend Charles Canfield to put up $400 for a three-acre parcel of land near downtown Los Angeles (Davis 1998).

The two men began sinking a shaft by hand at a site close to where present-day Glendale Boulevard approaches Second Street. At a depth of 7 feet, they encountered a seep of light oil. A bit deeper, the oil-soaked shale crackled from bubbling gas. At 155 feet, the two men had to stop digging because they could no longer bear the fumes. They then used a sharpened eucalyptus tree as a makeshift drill bit and struck oil and gas in November 1892. Doheny and

Canfield had discovered the Los Angeles City oil field and triggered a land boom (Testa 2005).

By mid-1894, the field was producing about 120 barrels per day. Between 1892 and 1900, almost a thousand wells were drilled in the area. Doheny went on to discover oil throughout the Los Angeles basin, southern California, and Mexico and become an important force in the global oil industry. In 1925 the Standard Oil Company of Indiana (later Amoco) acquired a controlling interest in Doheny's operations outside California. Valued at nearly $38.6 million, the deal was the largest transaction of its type up to that time.

The First Offshore Wells in the United States

In 1896 the first salt-water offshore wells in the United States were drilled over the water close to the shore, to exploit an offshore extension of the Summerland oil field in Santa Barbara County, on land owned by Henry Lafayette Williams. The drilling rigs were installed on a pier known as Treadwell Wharf, built by railroad engineer J.B. Treadwell. The furthest wells from shore were under about twenty-five feet of water at low tide (Grosbard 2002).

Giant Fields

California today has seventeen giant fields, fifteen predominantly oil and two predominantly natural gas. Four of these fields were discovered in the nineteenth century (see table 1.1). These were Brea (1884), Coalinga (1887), Kern River (1899), and Midway-Sunset (1894). Midway-Sunset would go on to become the fourth-largest field in the United States. It is a complex of twenty-two identifiable pools, located northwest of Los Angeles in Kern County. Discoveries in the Sunset part of the complex date back to 1894, when Jewett and Blodgett drilled sixteen wells that averaged a total production of 30 barrels per day of heavy oil. Development accelerated after 1900, with discoveries in the Midway part of the complex. The Midway-Sunset complex had produced a total of 2.4 billion barrels by 1999. With an estimated ultimate recovery of about 3.4 billion barrels, it still has not reached the end of its useful life.

THE OPENING OF THE MID-CONTINENT

The Mid-Continent Oil Region of the United States does not have precise boundaries. It is an aggregation of oil-producing areas spanning the states of Arkansas, Kansas, Nebraska, Oklahoma, Louisiana, New Mexico, and Texas (Wells and Wells 2021a, although the last three states mentioned are omitted in some definitions). In the twentieth century, it became arguably the most important oil region in the world, until the development of oil in the Middle East, and it played a crucial role in enabling allied victory in two world wars. In the nineteenth century, though, it was in its infancy.

Kansas

The Mid-Continent Oil Region opened up in Kansas, with the Norman No. 1 Well near Neodesha, on November 28, 1892, drilled by Albert P. McBride and Camden L. Bloom, approximately 150 miles southwest of Kansas City. However, the 832-foot-deep Norman No.1 was not the first well drilled in Kansas. The first wells were drilled in 1860 near the town of Paola, between Neodesha and Kansas City, because of oil seeps observed along Wea Creek. There was also a gas discovery in Iola, not far from Neodesha, with a 737-foot-deep well in 1873. In 1886, a small refinery was established (Merriam 2002).

The 1892 Norman No. 1 Well attracted attention from a number of experienced oilmen, including James M. Guffey and John H. Galey (Flaherty 2010). In 1897 Standard Oil completed a refinery in Neodesha. In the early twentieth century, Kansas's Eldorado Field, discovered in 1915, would play an important role in supplying the Allies during the First World War.

Oklahoma

The state of Oklahoma was not admitted to the Union until 1907. Before then, its area was composed of the Oklahoma Territory and Indian Territory, of which the Cherokee Nation controlled a portion in the northeast. In 1884 the Cherokee Nation passed a law authorizing the "organization of a company for the purpose of finding petroleum, or rock oil, and thus increasing the revenue of the Cherokee Nation." In 1889 Edward Byrd obtained Cherokee mineral leases and drilled Oklahoma's first intentional oil well near Chelsea in 1890. The well, flowing at half a barrel per day, was not commercially successful (Skelton 2006).

On April 15, 1897, Albert P. McBride and Camden L. Bloom—the same pair that drilled Norman No. 1 in Kansas—completed Oklahoma's first commercial oil well near the new small town of Bartlesville, on behalf of the Cudahy Oil Company. The well, Nellie Johnstone No. 1, was named for the six-year-old daughter of William Johnstone, a Cudahy partner, and was the discovery well of the large Bartlesville-Dewey field. It was a gusher flowing up to seventy-five barrels a day. Because of the lack of storage tanks and railroad connections, the well had to be capped for two years (Skelton 2006).

The Bartlesville-Dewey field would be the largest ever found in Oklahoma. It became profitable in 1900, when rail transportation became available in the area. Bartlesville-Dewey did not immediately achieve its full potential or initiate an immediate boom, but by 2002 it had produced 1.5 billion barrels.

After the turn of the century, in 1905, the Glenn Pool was discovered (Hyne 2015). Although smaller than Bartlesville-Dewey, it was quicker to be exploited and initiated a major industry boom. When Oklahoma became a state in 1907, it was the top-producing state in the United States. It would trade places with California for the leading position in the early years of the twentieth century. In 1928 both were overtaken by Texas.

Texas

Texas, the most prolific producing state in the United States for over a century until the present day, was almost insignificant in the 1800s.

Early Developments

The first well known to have been purposely drilled for oil was by Lyne T. Barret. He leased 279 acres near Oil Springs in Nacogdoches County on December 15, 1859. The Civil War interrupted his work for several years, but on December 21, 1865, he organized the Melrose Petroleum Company with Benjamin P. Hollingsworth, Charles A. Hamilton, John T. Flint, and John B. Earle. On September 12, 1866, he made a modest strike at 106 feet, producing about 10 barrels per day He obtained the services of geologist John F. Carll (see chapter 7) to test and develop the field. Although indications were positive, a combination of low oil prices and the uncertainties associated with Reconstruction made it impossible to obtain financing. The field would remain undeveloped until 1887, when others would exploit it (Devereaux 1995).

Corsicana

The Corsicana oil field, found in 1894, is generally considered the first truly commercial discovery in Texas. The following account is taken largely from Smith (1952). The town of Corsicana in 1890 was a cotton-processing and trade center. Its civic leaders wanted to diversify the industrial base and determined that better water supplies were necessary. While drilling for water, the contractor, American Well and Prospecting Company, discovered oil on June 9, 1894. On September 6, local citizens Ralph Beaton and H.G. Damon organized the Corsicana Oil Development Company with John Davidson, a Pennsylvania oil entrepreneur, and leased oil rights near the well.

In 1895 Corsicana Oil Development entered into an agreement with the Guffey and Galey Company of Pittsburgh (Flaherty 2010). Guffey and Galey, experienced oilmen, agreed to drill five test wells and would obtain a half interest in the leases of the Corsicana company. By August 1896, four of the five wells were producing in small quantities, averaging 20–40 barrels per day. This led to an oil boom, which was unfortunately chaotic and wasteful, with wells too closely spaced. Guffey and Galey sold their interest to local investors in September 1897.

Drilling and production in the Corsicana field continued. Production increased sharply from 1,450 barrels in 1896 to 65,974 barrels in 1897. In 1898 the field expanded to encompass a broader area of the countryside surrounding Corsicana, and production shot up to 546,070 barrels. By 1993 the Corsicana field had produced 44 million barrels of oil. Joseph S. Cullinan, the future founder of the Texas Company (later Texaco), visited Corsicana in 1897 to inspect the oil field at the invitation of the mayor. He stayed and formed the J.S. Cullinan Company, which would later form part of the Magnolia Petroleum Company (eventually part of Mobil).

Spindletop

Corsicana established Texas as an oil state. The Spindletop discovery, just after the turn of the century, in 1901, established it as a future world leader. The field was discovered on January 10 near the town of Beaumont, by Anthony F. Lucas. Lucas followed the vision of Pattillo Higgins, the "prophet of Spindletop," who became convinced in the 1880s that there was oil to be found there when the conventional wisdom disagreed. The Spindletop oil discovery spawned or nurtured several major petroleum companies and initiated a petroleum boom in Texas. Spindletop is often considered to mark the transition from the petroleum industry's focus on illumination to its modern focus on transportation fuel.

The Spindletop field was discovered in the formations surrounding a salt-dome structure. The first unsuccessful wells at Spindletop were drilled using cable-tool equipment. Anthony F. Lucas's successful discovery well was drilled using a more modern rotary tool. Lucas's well was a gusher struck at 1,139 feet. It blew a column of oil 100 feet high and was not brought under control until nine days later (Wooster and Sanders 1976). Spindletop as a whole produced nearly 48,000 barrels per day in 1902. By the end of 1902, the population of Beaumont grew from 8,000 to 60,000 (Douet 2020). By 1904 production was down to 10,000 barrels per day. Principles of reservoir management and conservation were not yet well developed, and too many wells had been drilled in the shallow caprock. Lucas reportedly said that "the cow was milked too hard; moreover, she was not milked intelligently." Production thereafter was somewhat better controlled. By 1985 the field had produced more than 153 million barrels and was soon exhausted. It was nowhere near being Texas's most important field and did not even meet the criteria for being a giant; however, its historical importance was seminal.

More than 600 companies were formed or had major operations at Spindletop; some would become giants of the modern international petroleum industry (Vassiliou 2018):

- The Guffey Petroleum Company and the Gulf Refining Company of Texas were both born at Spindletop (Mann 2011). They later became Gulf Oil (eventually merged with Chevron).
- The Texas Company (later Texaco, eventually joined with Chevron) was also established at Spindletop, by the same Joseph Cullinan who had formed one of the antecedent companies of Mobil at Corsicana (see earlier).
- The Humble Oil and Refining Company (acquired by Standard Oil Company of New Jersey, later Exxon, and eventually, ExxonMobil) was founded by families connected with Spindletop.
- Sun Oil Company, eventually to be known as Sunoco, had roots dating back to 1886 in the Lima-Indiana field. Sun operated at Spindletop and built a major refinery at Marcus Hook, Pennsylvania, to process its crude.
- Edward Doheny's Pan-American Petroleum and Transport Company (later part of Standard Oil of Indiana, or Amoco) also had operations at Spindletop.
- The Shell Transport and Trading Company (later Royal Dutch Shell) played a role in transporting Spindletop oil to the United Kingdom.

BIG BUSINESS: STANDARD OIL

Standard Oil was the dominant oil company in the United States in the late nineteenth and early twentieth centuries and, in many ways, the dominant oil company in the world. Its influence would redound well into the twentieth century and beyond.

Early Years

Standard Oil was founded in 1870 by John D. Rockefeller and Henry Flagler as an Ohio joint stock company, headquartered in Cleveland. This first Standard Oil company of 1870 should not be confused with the later Standard Oil Company of Ohio (Sohio), an independent successor company formed after the breakup of the Standard Oil Trust in 1911.

Standard Oil had roots in a number of previous Rockefeller companies: Andrews, Clark and Company (1863), Rockefeller and Andrews (1865), and Rockefeller, Andrews, and Flagler (1867). The 1867 company united the refineries of Rockefeller & Andrews, S. V. Harkness, and Henry Flagler, among others. Rockefeller had a goal of horizontal integration to achieve economies of scale in refining, which in the 1860s was dominated by small firms. As he later put it himself: "The cause leading to the combination was the desire to unite our skill and capital, in order to carry on a business of some magnitude and importance in place of the small business that each had separately heretofore carried on" (Montague 1902, 267). Standard Oil was capitalized initially at $1 million (Montague 1902, 267). Rockefeller was president, and Flagler was secretary. Rockefeller owned 27 percent of the stock.

Horizontal Integration and Anticompetitive Practices

Standard Oil was already a powerful company when it was formed, and it continued to grow through a combination of shrewd management and the application of a number of anticompetitive practices. One of the levers Rockefeller used early on to gain control was to attempt to control the handling and transport of oil and oil products, which accounted for at least two-thirds of the cost of a barrel (Mayhew 2008, 15). Rockefeller negotiated special arrangements with railroads to his benefit, beginning in the 1860s.

From 1870 to 1872, Standard helped hatch a scheme, the "South Improvement Company," for American refining companies and railroads to collude and control the market for oil and its transport. The South Improvement Company was organized by Thomas Scott, soon-to-be head of the Pennsylvania Railroad, as a supposedly independent Pennsylvania corporation. South Improvement's shareholders were large refiners including Standard Oil and three railroads—the Pennsylvania, the Erie, and the New York Central and Hudson River. Refiners that were members of South Improvement would obtain preferential shipping rates from South Improvement's railroad members. The agreement was administered as a system of rebates paid to member refiners, but not to other customers who shipped petroleum products. The rebates could be substantial. In one locality, South Improvement paid an effective rate of $0.44 per barrel after the rebate, while Standard Oil's competitors paid $1.50.

In February 1872 the railroads doubled the freight rates for refiners that were not members of South Improvement. Standard Oil exploited the panic that ensued over the next two months and bought out twenty-two of its twenty-six competitors in the Cleveland refining industry, in what became known as the "Cleveland Massacre." Among the acquired companies was Standard Oil's largest competitor, Clark, Payne and Company. In what would become a recurring pattern, Rockefeller made one of the partners, Colonel Oliver Payne, an executive at Standard Oil.

Rockefeller invoked the specter of the South Improvement Company, and his own determination to control the industry, to bully refiners into being acquired. The journalist Ida Tarbell recounted that Rockefeller would tell his targets, "You see, this scheme is bound to work. It means an absolute control by us of the oil business. There is no chance for anyone outside. But we are going to give everybody a chance to come in. You are to turn over your refinery to my appraisers, and I will give you Standard Oil Company stock or cash, as you prefer, for the value we put upon it. I advise you to take the stock. It will be for your good" (Tarbell 1905, 63).

Standard also selectively lowered prices in markets where competitors operated, while keeping prices high elsewhere. It forced competitors to choose between going bankrupt or being acquired by Standard Oil. It also made some friendly acquisitions of companies eager to be affiliated with it. Standard was thus able to achieve significant horizontal integration of its operations. By 1880 Standard Oil controlled over 90 percent of refinery throughput in the United States. This percentage went down over the next two decades, but in the period from 1895 to 1897, it was still over 80 percent of a vastly increased base. This is shown in figure 5.6. As Standard dominated refining, the country moved from large numbers of small refineries to smaller numbers of large ones, with considerable increases in total throughput, as shown in figure 5.7.

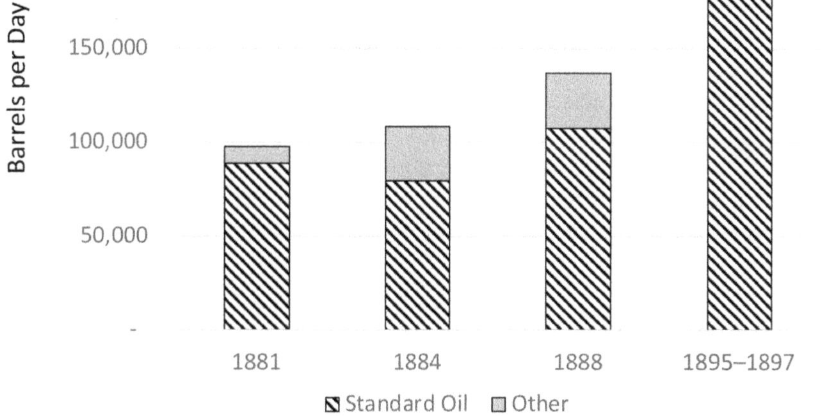

Figure 5.6. US Refinery Throughput in Barrels per Day, for Standard Oil and Other Companies. ***Source*****: From data in Williamson and Daum (1959, 473, 627).**

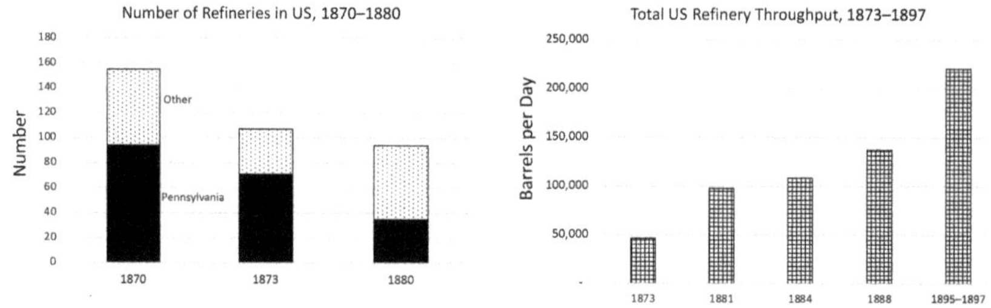

Figure 5.7. (Left) Number of Refineries in the United States, 1870–1880. (Right) US Refinery Throughput in Barrels per Day, 1873–1897. *Source*: From data in Williamson and Daum (1959, 473, 627).

Vertical Integration

At first, Standard concentrated almost exclusively on refining and did not move upstream into oil exploration and production, which Rockefeller considered risky endeavors. However, the company was not immune to the vagaries of crude oil supply, especially as the initial discoveries of the US oil industry in Pennsylvania began to run low. Eventually, it overcame its initial aversion to upstream operations. Rockefeller took a risk on the new Lima-Indiana oil field discovered in 1886 in northwestern Ohio and later in Indiana. The oil had a high sulfur content, making its refined products foul smelling and unsuitable for use in lamps, as we have already observed earlier in this chapter. Standard Oil marketed the oil as fuel oil, but there was no guarantee that it would ever be usable for illumination.

Rockefeller consulted with Herman Frasch, who developed a process to desulfurize the oil (chapter 7). Standard completed a large refinery at Whiting, Indiana, near Chicago, in 1890 to refine Lima crude, and it soon converted other refineries to do so. Lima crude represented a competitive advantage for Standard Oil once it had the Frasch process. It could now produce refined products competitive with those derived from Pennsylvania-Appalachian oil, but using cheaper, lower-quality Lima oil as an input. Once Standard had begun upstream integration with its purchase of Lima properties, it continued the process with Appalachian properties. By 1891 Standard held properties producing about a quarter of the US national output of crude.

Backlash, Counterreactions, and Breakup

Standard's practices enraged the upstream producers in the Pennsylvania Oil Regions, and they boycotted refiners and railroads. South Improvement lost its charter in April 1872, about three months after it had been granted. The US Congress launched an investigation, and John D. Rockefeller was publicly identified as the mastermind behind the scheme. Despite the collapse of South Improvement, Rockefeller had achieved his primary purpose, which was to buy out his competition. Standard Oil and the railroads also continued to negotiate in secret, and Standard Oil continued to obtain preferential rates.

The crude oil producers in western Pennsylvania struck back at Standard by forming the Tidewater Pipeline Company and completing a pipeline in 1879 connecting the oil regions with the Reading Railroad, which did not carry oil at the time and which was not allied with Standard (Chandler 1977, 322; see also chapter 7). Tidewater extended its pipeline to the east coast of the United States, further threatening Standard's control of transport, given that pipeline transport was also more efficient than rail. Standard Oil responded by building its own pipelines from the oil regions east to the coast and west to Cleveland. Standard also extracted leverage from the fact that it controlled the refiners to whom Tidewater was delivering oil. Standard Oil survived the backlash from its competitors, but it would ultimately not survive the interventions of the government, at least not in the same corporate form.

In foreign markets, Standard Oil faced considerable competition from Branobel and the Rothschilds (see chapter 6) beginning in the 1880s and from Royal Dutch and Shell beginning in the 1890s. It waged price wars against all these major foreign competitors, but it was unable to bankrupt them or buy them out. Royal Dutch and Shell instead later combined with each other to form the Royal Dutch Shell group in 1907.

In 1882 Rockefeller created the Standard Oil Trust, headquartered in New York City. The trust united Standard Oil (Ohio) and various affiliated companies under one umbrella. It held "in trust" all the assets of the various Standard Oil companies. The structure, which was the first major implementation of the trust-type arrangement in the United States, was deliberately confusing and opaque, to discourage public scrutiny.

Standard Oil's size and power led to public hostility and helped prompt the passage of the Sherman Antitrust Act in 1890. The act prohibited various activities restricting interstate commerce and market competition. That year, the state of Ohio sued Standard Oil for illegal monopolization of the petroleum industry. On March 2, 1892, the Ohio Supreme Court convicted Standard Oil of violating the Sherman Antitrust Act by forming a holding company, interpreted as being a conspiracy in restraint of trade. Despite the Ohio court ruling, and continuing legal attempts to stop it, the trust continued to operate for several years.

Eventually, Standard Oil took advantage of favorable New Jersey laws allowing corporations to hold stock in other corporations. In 1899 it renamed its New Jersey firm Standard Oil Company (New Jersey) and placed it at the hub of the organization. Assets that were formerly in the Standard Oil Trust were put into the holding company. The various Standard Oil companies continued to function effectively as a single entity, through interlocking directorates and various other complex arrangements. Despite the New Jersey charter, Standard Oil continued to be run from New York. By this time Rockefeller was secretly retired, and the company was being run largely by John Archbold.

The discovery at Spindletop in 1901 ushered in new competitors for Standard, including the future Texaco and Gulf, as petroleum's age of illumination gave way to its age of energy, and gasoline replaced kerosene as the most important refined product. In addition to the increased competition, Standard also faced continuing legal challenges. In November 1906 US attorney general George Wickersham brought charges against the company for monopoly and restraint of trade in the Federal Circuit Court of the Eastern District of Missouri. The case, prosecuted by Frank Billings Kellogg, lasted three years. In 1909 the court found Standard Oil (New Jersey) guilty of violating the

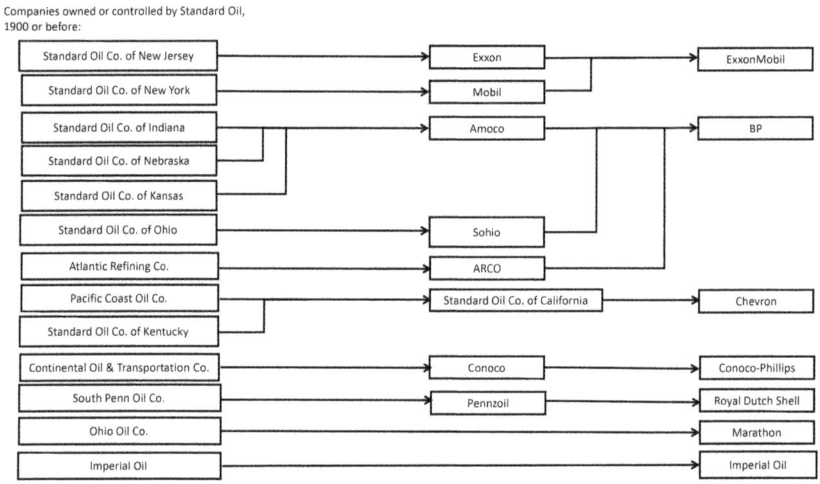

Figure 5.8. Descendants of the Various Companies Owned or Controlled by Standard Oil in the Nineteenth Century. Many of today's most important private-sector oil companies have significant Standard Oil heritage. ExxonMobil is probably the company whose lineage traces most directly to Standard Oil. Chevron would also be a more or less direct descendant, except that it acquired significant non-Standard heritage when it merged with Texaco in 2001. BP had its own non-Standard lineage via the Anglo-Persian and Anglo-Iranian oil companies, but acquired considerable Standard Oil heritage when it acquired Sohio in 1987, merged with Amoco in 1998, and acquired ARCO in 2000. Conoco was a direct descendant of Standard Oil but acquired non-Standard heritage when it merged with Phillips Petroleum in 2002. Royal Dutch Shell obtained a relatively small amount of Standard heritage when it acquired part of Pennzoil in 2002 (mainly the motor oil brand). *Source*: from information in Vassiliou (2018).

Sherman Antitrust Act by forming a holding company and by restraining competition among merged firms by fixing transportation costs, supply costs, and prices. Standard Oil appealed to the US Supreme Court, which upheld the ruling on May 15, 1911. A short time later, the Supreme Court ordered Standard Oil dissolved into thirty-four independent companies. Far from being a disaster for John D. Rockefeller, this event turned him from a millionaire to the world's first billionaire. An authoritative biography of Rockefeller can be found in Chernow (1998).

Standard Oil was the direct ancestor of several of the major oil companies that controlled the global oil market for a large part of the twentieth century and still exert considerable influence today. Figure 5.8 illustrates the staggering number of today's top oil companies with Standard Oil heritage. Among the companies formed by the dissolution of Standard Oil were many that would continue to be giants in the global petroleum industry: Standard Oil of New Jersey, or Jersey Standard (later Exxon and ExxonMobil); Standard Oil Company of New York (Socony, later Mobil and ExxonMobil); Vacuum Oil Company (later Mobil and ExxonMobil); Standard Oil of Indiana (later Amoco, eventually merged into BP); Standard Oil of California (later Chevron); Atlantic Refining Company (later Atlantic Richfield, or ARCO, eventually acquired by BP); Continental Oil Company (later Conoco and ConocoPhillips); South Penn Oil Company (later Pennzoil, eventually acquired in part by Royal Dutch Shell); Standard Oil Company of Ohio (Sohio, eventually acquired by BP); and, Ohio Oil Company (later Marathon). Of these, Jersey Standard was by far the largest, with about 43 percent of the assets of the original company. The second largest, Socony, had less than 5 percent. The newly independent companies were not functionally integrated, and many found themselves with refining and marketing capacity but no sources of crude. In the aftermath of the breakup, Jersey Standard, Socony, and others embarked on acquisition programs to gain control of crude reserves.

Chapter 6

Nineteenth-Century Oil in Azerbaijan

The Azerbaijani industry from the early 1800s onward differed markedly from the American one in that it was far more strictly controlled by the government. In America, private landholders owned significant subsurface mineral rights, and the acquisition of leases and rights involved transactions between private parties. In Tsarist Azerbaijan, the government controlled all the rights to exploit oil, and it either administered that exploitation itself or allowed others to do so—inefficiently before 1872, and more efficiently thereafter.

In chapter 4 we discussed the 1846 well and some of the activity preceding it. Here, we will discuss the Azerbaijani industry after 1846 but also provide additional details on the period before 1846. Figure 6.1 depicts the rough geographic location of oil-bearing areas in the Absheron peninsula.

GOVERNMENT OWNERSHIP AND MONOPOLISTIC LEASE-OUT

As Russia incorporated Azerbaijan into its empire, oil wells became the property of the imperial government. The government established a lease-out system, whereby wells could be leased out to a party who would operate them on a monopolistic basis. The Absheron oil wells operated under monopolistic lease-out during three distinct time periods: from 1806 through 1824, 1826 through 1834, and 1850 through 1872. From 1806 to 1824, the leaseholder in Baku was M.M. Tarumov, the secretary of the province; the last monopolistic leaseholder was I.M. Mirzoyev, from 1863 to 1872, when the system was abolished in favor of something much closer to free-market competition. General N.F. Rtischev, commander in chief in the Caucasus, produced a

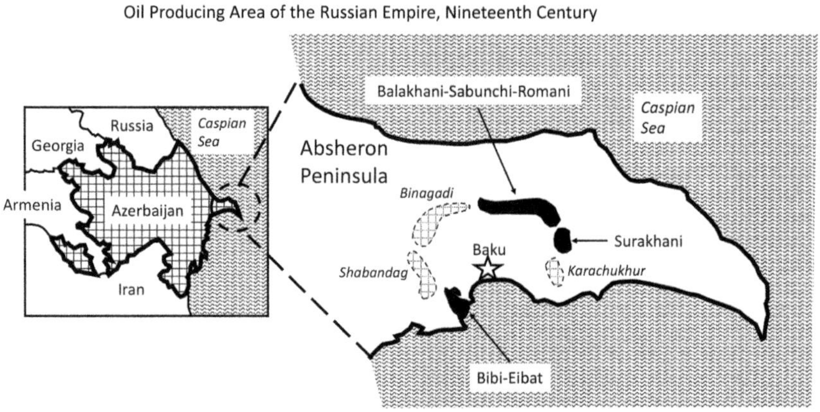

Figure 6.1. Generalized Sketch Map Showing the Rough Extent and Location (in Black) of the Three Nineteenth-Century Oil Field Complexes of Bibi-Eibat, Balakhani-Sabunchi-Romani, and Surakhani on the Absheron Peninsula of Azerbaijan. These accounted for essentially the entire oil production of the Russian Empire before 1900. Also shown, bounded by dotted lines are three major fields discovered in the twentieth century: Shabandag, Binagadi, and Karachukhur. These are included to illustrate the ring of producing structures surrounding the city of Baku. *Source*: Drawn using information in Tiratsoo (1984) and Griffiths et al. (2001).

report dated July 30, 1813, describing the Treasury's revenues from oil wells and various duties, and also indicating that "during four years of the lease-out system, this sector including other non-important sectors has brought 450 thousand rubles from procedures without taking any additional care or [requiring investment] by the Treasury" (Mir-Babayev 2008, 13).

It is worth noting that besides the resources in the Absheron peninsula, oil in small quantities was extracted in the Guba and Shirvan *uyezds* (districts) of Azerbaijan. Oil wells became the property of the Treasury and were put under the lease-out system as soon as those uyezds became part of Russia. The Guba Town Mayor who leased out wells had to make sure that "oil extraction did not rise arbitrarily. . . . Otherwise, it could damage the business of the most important Baku oil fields which were more useful for the Treasury than the oil in Guba" (Mir-Babayev 2008, 13).

The Russian Imperial Treasury strictly controlled the actions of the monopolistic leaseholder and forbade anyone other than the leaseholder to sell oil. As an example, Item 6 of the contract concluded between the Treasury and Tarumov in 1821 stipulates:

> Anyone caught breaking this rule . . . will be fined one thousand rubles for the first offense, in the form of State banknotes in favor of the Treasury and all quantities of oil put on sale by him will be transferred in favor of the leaseholder

> as the owner of oil, but once the second or the third illegal sale of oil occurs afterwards, besides all penalties in favor of the Treasury and leaseholder, the illegal merchant will be prosecuted in accordance with the laws (SHA-Azerbaijan-a, 24).

This contract gave guarantees to the monopolistic leaseholder for almost everything: manpower for digging and repairing wells; dredging oil out of wells; transporting it to city warehouses; and, the right to dig and search for new sources of oil. In return, the leaseholder had to pay large sums to the Treasury.

The monopolistic lease-out system had both advocates and detractors. One of the most ardent advocates was General N.F. Rtischev, who considered the lease-out system advantageous to the Treasury compared to direct government operation of wells. He wrote in his report dated July 30, 1813: "A true revenue for the Treasury from this sector may be ensured only if such wealth in abundance will be continuously leased out by honest people. . . . But once such fields are the permanent property of the Treasury, it will mean that there should be a special number of personnel with relevant salaries, as well as fees for workers and their visits. All of this requires significant expenditures from the Treasury" (Mir-Babayev 2008, 14). He was fully supported by Senator P.P. Gagarin.

Opponents of the system included Superintendent Reut of the Baku oil fields, Eduard Eichwald, state secretary F.P. Vronchenko, oilman V.I. Ragozin, and scientist Dmitri Mendeleev, among others. They preferred direct state administration of Baku's oil fields, as occurred in 1825, and from 1835 to 1849. For example, F.P. Vronchenko, in an October 12, 1844 letter to General A.I. Neidhardt, commander in chief of the Trans-Caucasus, wrote: "Oil export to Persia was not less if we compare the first eight years from 1828 to 1836 with the second eight years from 1836 to 1844. . . . [O]n the contrary, it had an increase of 9,139 poods. . . . Net revenues of the Treasury for the three full years of 1840, 1841 and 1842 were running up to 109 thousand rubles. The last lease-out sum in total was equal to 91 thousand rubles" (Mir-Babayev 2008, 14).

NIKOLAI VOSKOBOINIKOV, 1825–1846

The oil fields were under direct government administration in the year 1825, when the engineer Nikolai Voskoboinikov of the Tsar's Mining Expedition, along with his mission-mate Praporshik Talalayev, was sent to Baku to

> check and accept: Baku's major wells and warehouses with white and black oils as public property located in Balakhani, Binagadi, Surakhani and Bake from

> Tarumov. Leaseholders should present a detailed, commonly-signed registration book [describing] the number of wells and warehouses, their status, and quantities of unsold oil still stored at warehouses; which buildings and assets belonging to the leaseholder should be handed over to the Treasury; how much unsold and stored oil in Masazyr and Zykh is in Baku; whether the warehouses are appropriate for use (SHA-Azerbaijan-b, 2).

After completing his assessment, Voskoboinikov sent an extensive report to the Mining Expedition about the status of oil and salt resources in the Absheron. His materials remain the only comprehensive description of the status of the public and private oil wells of the Absheron under the monopolistic lease-out system, on the eve of its transition to direct state administration. According to Voskoboinikov, there were seventeen wells near Bibi-Eibat on January 1, 1825, leased out by Tarumov, along with one private well and eighty-two public wells with black oil in Balakhani. Voskoboinikov underlined that there were sixteen stone warehouses constructed alongside the northern ramparts of Baku city, full of oil transported on carts from almost all of the oil wells of the Absheron. (Currently, these warehouse sites are used for the building housing the Presidium of the National Academy of Sciences, called "Ismailliya," and M. A. Sabir Square).

Voskoboinikov noted the following in 1827:

> The peninsula of the Absheron represents woodless and almost fruitless lands. . . . But nature has filled the gaps of this country by forming in its terrestrial bowels abundant sources of oil and salt which meet not only the needs of the local residents, but also serve as a prerequisite of their wealth. . . . But what is black oil—black tar? It is in the entrails of the earth, but it seeps out to the surface of this ancient land in various altitudes and even on the seabed (Mir-Babayev 2008, 15).

Voskoboinikov was the director of the Baku oil and salt fields in 1825 and between 1834 and 1838. Both periods were ones of direct state administration of oil. He had a major impact on the extraction, exploration, storage, and sale of oil. The wealthy and powerful elites of the area were against direct government administration. Such people included Y.F. Kankrin, minister of finance; General E.A. Golovkin, commander in chief in the Caucasus who had replaced General A.P. Yermosol; and others. Despite obstacles they placed in his way, Voskoboinikov undertook a number of actions to advance the Absheron oil industry: concreting of pavement at oil warehouses; the beginnings of refining techniques to obtain kerosene from Surakhani oil; registration and tracking of oil storage; use of white and black oil instead of turpentine, tar, and cod-liver oil for lighting street lamps, lighthouses, and private homes; and using oil to treat timber for better ship construction.

As early as 1834, Voskoboinikov wrote a report to Minister Kankrin advising in situ refining of kerosene: "It will be useful to refine crude oil by distillation at the immediate site [of extraction], which would lower costs for the state treasury because there are some natural fires available near the wells of white oil" (ACAC 1884, 651). However, this report was ignored. In 1837 Voskoboinikov spearheaded the Trans-Caucasus Society for the Promotion of Industry and Trade, facilitating data collection on oil consumption in the entire Caucasus. Voskoboinikov's refinery became the first such plant in the Absheron, constructed in Balakhani in 1837 (ACAC 1884, 651).

As we noted in chapter 4, Voskoboinikov was an early proponent of drilling for oil, as opposed to gathering it from hand-dug wells. He was an intellectual force behind the 1846 well but was not directly involved in the execution. He resigned in 1846 and left the Absheron forever.

AFTER THE 1846 WELL

After the 1846 well discussed in chapter 4, the industry would mostly languish under old management habits. There was another well drilled by the government in 1848, yielding 110 poods (about twelve barrels) per day. However, as time went on, the government made no attempt to continue the modernization initiatives conceived by Voskoboinikov, and championed by Semyonov (chapter 4). The government, especially Grand Duke Mikhail Vorontsov, supported the monopolistic lease-out system, and in 1850 another such lease-out regime was established that would last until 1872. Leaseholders could obtain renewable four-year monopoly contracts. The monopolistic lease holders from 1850 to 1863 were M. Tarumov, A. Yakubov, and A. Akhmedov. From 1863 to 1872, it was I. M. Mirzoyev. The Tsarist government officially forbade additional competitive exploration and development.

It was not until the oil industry in the United States boomed after the 1859 Drake well that Russian official attitudes began to change. After a visit to the Paris International Exhibition in 1867, where he probably viewed drilling equipment from the United States, the great chemist Dmitri Mendeleev criticized the monopolistic lease-out system for its lack of proper incentives to move the industry forward. He said leaseholders "do not have any incentive to establish large-scale businesses as their rent has a short-term character. They are not interested in investing capital in exploration and test drilling: they do not want to dig nine wells to find the tenth successful one that will cover their expenses. Perhaps this tenth one will only be found when the term of their rent is over, or is so close that the [leaseholder] would not enjoy to the full the results of his entrepreneurship" (Moser 2018, 19).

In the late 1860s there was some drilling. Russia's first post-1846 drilled well, in 1864, was not actually in Azerbaijan, but in the Kudako River region in Kuban, under the supervision of Colonel Ardalion Novosiltsev. It reached a depth of 650 feet (Fooks and Matishev 2000, 137). In 1869 monopolistic leaseholder I.M. Mirzoyev drilled a 210-foot well in Balakhani that proved to be a dry hole. In 1871 he drilled a second one to a depth of 147 feet in the same area and struck oil. The well yielded an average of 240 barrels per day. However, the big explosion in drilling and production would only take place after the reforms of 1872.

THE REFORMS OF 1872

On February 1, 1872, Tsar Alexander II approved the proposed regulatory framework "On Rules in the Oil Business and Excise from the . . . Production" in Saint Petersburg by writing the following resolution on the document presented to him—"So be it!" (Gorny 1872, 20; RGRI 2021). This gave the green light for Russian, local and foreign, capital to invest in Azerbaijani oil.

The building blocks of the 1872 reforms began to be laid in 1867, when two special commissions were established. One was within the Russian Ministry of Finance in Saint Petersburg and was chaired by Duke N.M. Leihtenbergskiy. The other was chaired by I.A. Shteiman, the chief of mining in the Caucasus region, and was located in Tiflis. The Shteiman Commission recommended major free-market reforms: the abolition of the short-term monopolistic lease-out system and the establishment of auctions to sell long-term leases to small plots of one desyatin (2.7 acres) to multiple private entrepreneurs. It also recommended that oil production be free of excise taxes. The Shteiman Commission's recommendations were reviewed by the Leihtenbergskiy Commission, which mostly approved them. The Leihtenbergskiy Commission increased the size of the plots to ten desyatins (27 acres) and reduced the excise tax rather than abolishing it (Moser 2018, 19; note that Moser refers to Shteiman as "Steinman").

Before it could auction off plots, the government needed to develop systematic knowledge about known oil deposits, existing wells, and their geographic distribution. Engineer Gilev carried out a survey for the Mining Administration in Tiflis, which published the information in 1871. The auction was organized for forty-eight twenty-seven-acre plots. The February 1, 1872, regulations contained a number of provisos. For example, no leaseholder could have two plots that were too close together; they had to be separated by at least two versts (about 1.3 miles). The opening price of a plot in the auction, and its rent after acquisition, was calculated based on the level of existing production. How a plot was worked was left largely to the holder, but work had to begin within two years of acquisition. If the holder did not pay his rent, he could forfeit the plot (Moser 2018, 22).

Four weekly auctions were held beginning December 7, 1872. All the plots were sold off, generating 2.98 million rubles—over five times the sum of minimum bids. The excess payments were largely due to a competition over the first four plots, which had the greatest current production and were thus deemed the most desirable. Based on the very useful detailed tabulation of the auction results in Moser (2018, 20–21), the team of V.A. Kokorev and P.I. Gubonin acquired the top two plots, paying premiums of 124 percent and 349 percent, respectively, over asking price. This stimulated their main competitor, I.M. Mirzoyev—the last monopolistic leaseholder under the old system—to overpay outrageously for the plot with the third-largest current production, a premium of 707 percent over asking. The top four plots garnered 2.05 million rubles, or 68.8 percent of the total. The Kokorev/Gubonin team and Mirzoyev dominated the top-producing properties. The two competitive parties acquired 91 percent of current production and paid 86 percent of the total moneys that went into the tsar's coffers in the auction. The rest of the blocks went to a variety of other parties, including Z. Tagiyev, who would become wildly successful in future.

THE RESULTS OF THE 1872 REFORMS: EXPLOSIVE DEVELOPMENT

A glance at table D.1 or figure 1.1 reveals the results of the 1872 reforms: an explosion in production. The production of Azerbaijani oil in 1873 was 2.57 times the level in 1872. By 1880 production was over 16 times the 1872 level, and by 1900 it was more than 400 times. A succession of impressive gushers ensued in the Absheron peninsula. The first, Vermishevskiy, was struck by the Khalafi Trading Society on June 13, 1873: more than 90 million poods of oil (~10.8 million barrels) were collected in three months. On October 14, 1875, a second gusher was struck by the Souchastniki Company at a depth of 315 feet, yielding up to 150,000 poods (~24,000 barrels) a day in the first month (Mir-Babayev 2008, 19).

After the auctions, activity began promptly, and operators generally wasted little time in adopting drilling techniques, largely abandoning the old practice of digging wells by hand. According to the data of S.M. Lisichkin, the overall number of functioning wells in 1873 was equal to 158, with only 9 of them drilled, but by 1876 there were 62 drilled wells out of a total of 124. In 1878 there were 301 drilled oil wells in the Absheron, 251 of which were located in the greater Balakhani complex (Mir-Babayev 2008, 19).

In 1873 an engineer named V. Neruchev visited Baku and noted the manner of oil extraction from drilled wells:

> [T]he spoon lifts almost 5–8 poods [between half a barrel and a barrel] of oil, which takes from 45 seconds to three minutes depending on the depth of the well and how the movement is powered. If [the operation] is performed using steam power and the well depth does not exceed 30 sazhens [210 feet], then one lifting and lowering of the spoon need not take more than 45 seconds; [. . . using] horse power, it takes almost a minute; [and using] manpower, it takes approximately 2–3 minutes. This method of oil extraction is in Baku is called oil-bailing (Mir-Babayev 2008, 19).

Oil Was Poured into a Trough Leading to Storage Areas. The post-1872 regulatory regime led to the creation of many oil companies and trading firms, including the firm of H.Z. Tagiyev (1872); the Baku Oil Society (1874); the Nobel Brothers Co. (1879); the Caspian and Black Sea Society of the Rothschilds (1883); Oil (1883); the firm of S.M. Shibayev (1884); the Caspian Company (1887); the firm of Naghiyev Musa (1887); the firm of A.I. Mantashev (1899); the firm of Shamsi Asadullayev (1893); Caucasus (1896); the firm of I.A. Akhverdov (1896); Mazut (1898); Russian Oil Petroleum and Liquid Fuel Company (1898); Souchastniki (co-participants) (1899); the Absheron Oil Society (1899); the firm of Alexander Benkendorf (1900); Bibi-Eibat Petroleum Co. (1900); and the Balakhani Syndicate (1900).

BIG BUSINESS: THE NOBELS, THE ROTHSCHILDS, AND OTHERS

The Azerbaijani industry was never as thoroughly dominated by one company as the US industry was dominated by Standard Oil in its heyday. However, a few big companies had an outsize share of production and revenue. Figure 6.2 shows various companies' share of Azerbaijani oil production in 1900. The clear leaders were the Nobel Brothers, the Baku Oil Society, the Tagiyev firm, the Mantashev firm, the Caspian and Black Sea Oil Company of the Rothschilds, and the Caspian Company; together they accounted for nearly 48 percent of all production. We briefly delve into the most important companies in the following sections.

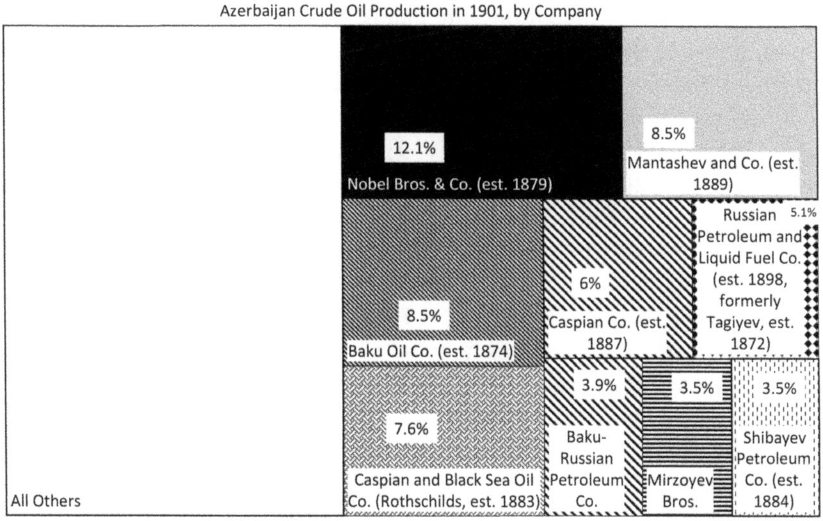

Figure 6.2. Azerbaijan Crude Oil Production in 1901, by Company. The top nine companies accounted for 58.6 percent of the total production of approximately 86.2 million barrels. The top producer, Nobel Brothers, accounted for 12.1 percent, with Mantashev and the Baku Oil Society second at 8.5 percent each. *Source*: Data from Thompson (1904, 120–122). Dates of establishment of companies are from Mir-Babayev (2011) and Moser (2018).

THE NOBEL COMPANY (BRANOBEL)

The Nobel Brothers Petroleum Production Company was a highly innovative oil company operating in Azerbaijan in the nineteenth and early twentieth centuries that played a major role in creating the Russian petroleum industry. It is often referred to as "Branobel," the shortened name for *Tovarishchestvo Nephtanavo Proisvodtsva Bratiev Nobel* (Nobel Brothers Petroleum Production Company), for cable communications. Ludvig Nobel headed the company from 1879 to 1888; his son Emanuel Nobel headed it from 1888 to 1920, when it was nationalized by the Bolsheviks. Useful accounts of Branobel's history can be found in many sources (Tolf 1976; Alekperov 2011; Moser 2018; Thompson 1904; Marvin 1891). Branobel was a vertically integrated oil company, spanning exploration and production, refining, transportation, and marketing.

The Nobels were a remarkable family, with many achievements to boast of both in and out of the petroleum industry. Ludvig's father, Immanuel, was a self-taught engineer who began a business in Saint Petersburg, Fonderies et Ateliers Mécaniques Nobel Fils, supplying the Russian military. He is credited with many inventions, including naval mines. Ludvig's brother, Alfred, invented dynamite and made a bequest establishing the Nobel Prize. Immanuel Nobel was brilliant but suffered financial difficulties. In 1833 he went bankrupt in Sweden and began a new business in Saint Petersburg, making equipment for the Russian Army. The business did very well for a time but faltered after the end of the Crimean War (1853–1856). The company's creditors appointed Ludvig Nobel to run it. Immanuel returned to Stockholm with his wife and his sons Emil and Alfred, while his other son Robert stayed behind to work with Ludvig. In Stockholm, Immanuel began experiments with nitroglycerine that killed his son Emil in 1864 but formed the basis for the work that later made Alfred famous.

Through great effort, Ludvig and Robert put the Saint Petersburg factory back on its feet. The Tsarist government, badly in need of modern small arms for its army, leased its Izhevsk Armory to the Nobels so that they could manufacture 200,000 rifles. At one point, Ludvig asked Robert to tour southern Russia in search of walnut for manufacturing stocks for the rifles. In 1873 Robert made his way to the Caucasus and eventually visited Baku, where he became interested in the oil industry there. Robert had already had some experience trading kerosene in Finland. He used the entire 25,000 rubles intended for the walnut purchase to buy some oil-bearing land and a refinery from the Dutch De Boer brothers.

Robert got the business started, and in 1876 Ludvig and his son, Emanuel, visited the Absheron peninsula. Ludvig began thinking strategically about the Baku oil industry and produced a memorandum, "A Look at the Baku Oil Industry and Its Future" (Alekperov 2011). He noted the experiences of the petroleum industry in the United States, which showed that the way to achieve profits was not to produce crude oil, but to refine it into kerosene for illumination. He identified the lack of effective transportation routes to get the Baku product to the rest of the world as a major problem and also noted that there was still a shortage of capital in Azerbaijan for investment in the industry. Ludvig proposed new methods, including pipelines, railroad tank cars, and ships, to replace the slow and inefficient use of ox-drawn carts to transport oil stored in wineskins. He also noted the need for storage tanks and for using residual heavy refinery fractions as fuel oil. He would eventually achieve all these goals.

Branobel was formally established as a joint stock company on May 18, 1879, after gaining imperial approval, with part of its stock listed on the Berlin Stock Exchange (Moser 2018, 31). Its initial capitalization was 3 million rubles. Ludvig Nobel invested 1.61 million rubles and had a controlling interest. Other investors were Alfred Nobel, with 115,000 rubles; Robert Nobel, 100,000 rubles; Peter Bilderling, 930,000 rubles; and some others (Alekperov 2011, 87).

Although Robert Nobel's first well at Sabunchi, in April 1876, was manually drilled, the company quickly adopted mechanized drilling methods and grew rapidly. In its first year, it accounted for about 5 percent of Russia's production. Two years later, in 1881, it accounted for 13.5 percent (Alekperov 2011, 88), and in 1890, 18.7 percent (Moser 2018, 36). In 1901, according to Thompson (1904, 120–122), Branobel accounted for 12.1 percent of Russian production, down in percentage terms but still the top company (see figure 6.2). Branobel's position was even more dominant as a kerosene producer; by 1883 it had 55 percent of the domestic market (Moser 2018, 38).

Branobel faced stiff competition from the Rothschilds as well as from independents such as Mantashev. The Rothschilds gained significant market share, but Branobel was more profitable. It invested more consistently and was more effectively integrated. Branobel encompassed exploration, production, refining, storage, transportation, and marketing. In 1878 the Nobels completed Russia's first pipeline, 5.6 miles long and three inches in diameter, with a capacity of nearly 10,000 barrels per day, and the company deployed the world's first modern oil tanker, the *Zoroaster*, which was designed by Ludvig Nobel (see also chapter 7). As pointed out by De Rudder (1997), Ludvig chose the tanker's name because of an interest he shared with many other educated people of the time, in Zoroastrian philosophy. The process of oil refining suggested parallels with Zoroastrianism's search for purity and sanctity.

By the mid-1880s, Branobel had a fleet of tankers transporting Baku oil across the Caspian, to be shipped on company ships and barges up the Volga River. In keeping with the theme of *Zoroaster*, Ludvig had a tendency to name his ships after religious leaders, philosophers, and scientists—for example, *Moses, Buddha, Mohammed, Spinoza, Darwin, Linnaeus, Nordenskjöld, Socrates, Koran, Talmud,* and *Calmuck*. Thanks again to _Ludvig's inventiveness, some of the company's tankers heated their boilers with a type of fuel oil when the rest of the world was using coal. Ludvig Nobel also developed a continuous distillation unit (chapter 7) incorporating ideas from Dmitri Mendeleev, and the company became the first in the world to perform continuous distillation on a large scale. The process produced higher kerosene yields (35 percent, according to Moser 2018, 43), and kerosene of a higher quality.

Emanuel Nobel continued in his father's innovative tradition, introducing rotary drilling techniques and building the world's first diesel engine plant. He installed diesel engines in power plants, tankers, tugboats, and pumping stations on the Baku-Batum Pipeline (chapter 7).

Branobel was also an exceptionally progressive employer by the standards of its time. Ludvig Nobel abolished child labor and shortened daily working hours from 14 to 10.5. He built decent housing for workers and provided them with free medical care, technical training, and elementary education for their children. He also created a cooperative bank for workers. With his brother Robert, he established a large park in Baku that still exists. While the Nobel Prize is today associated with the award established by Ludvig's brother Alfred, there was another Nobel Prize for a time in Russia, named after Ludvig. The Russian Imperial Technical Society awarded it beginning in 1896 for outstanding innovations in metallurgy or the oil industry. The prize consisted of a gold medal and the interest income on a principal of 6,000 rubles. A third Nobel Prize was named for Ludvig's son Emanuel (Mir-Babayev 2013; see also Appendix C).

As the nineteenth century turned to the twentieth, Russia edged toward the revolution of 1917. Unlike the Rothschilds, who sold out their interests to Royal Dutch Shell in 1912, the Nobels saw half of theirs nationalized by the Bolsheviks in 1920 (see section on nationalization). They managed to sell the other half to Standard Oil of New Jersey in May that year, just in the nick of time. Emanuel and his brothers were able to escape eventually to Sweden. They fought unsuccessfully for more than a decade to recover their assets from the Soviet government.

The Rothschild Company

The name of the Rothschild company in English was the Caspian and Black Sea Oil Production and Trading Company. In French, it was the Société Commerciale et Industrielle de Naphte Caspienne et de la Mer Noire; in Russian, it was Kaspiysko Chernjmjrskoe Neftepromushlenoe i Torgovoe Obchshestvo (KChNTO). The company has widely been referred to as BNITO, based on the Russian acronym of a predecessor company, the Batum Oil Production and Trading Company, which the Rothschilds took over in 1883 (Mir-Babayev 2012, 225).

From that toehold, the Rothschilds formed a larger company on July 30, 1885. In 1887 they also gained control of the Mazut Company, which concentrated on transporting and marketing oil and petroleum products. It had a fleet of tankers, with thirteen in the Caspian. Mazut also had a large fleet of barges and tugs carrying petroleum products up the Volga.

The Rothschilds presented stiff competition for the Nobel brothers' company Branobel, accounting for more than half of Russian kerosene exports by 1888. However, the Rothschild operation never achieved the same levels of profitability as that of the Nobels, as noted earlier. Unlike the vertically integrated Nobels, the Rothschilds concentrated on downstream operations and trading, especially in the early years. The Nobels also benefited from having acquired control of land earlier, when it was substantially cheaper.

The Rothschilds worked profitably with British industrialist Marcus Samuel, founder of the Shell Transport and Trading Company, which would later join with Royal Dutch to form Royal Dutch Shell. As the name of his company implied, Samuel's primary interest in the oil business was the transportation and marketing of products. He acquired a tanker fleet and in 1892 managed to obtain permission for his tankers to transit the Suez Canal. His were the first oil tankers to satisfy the Suez Canal Company of their safety and suitability. He was able to ship the Rothschilds' petroleum products efficiently from the Russian Empire to key Asian destinations such as Bangkok and Singapore. There they could be sold for less than Standard Oil products, which were burdened with higher transportation costs into Asian markets.

In 1903 the Rothschilds teamed with the Nobels to form a cartel, Nobmazut, to coordinate their efforts in the Russian domestic market. The Rothschilds sold their petroleum interests to Royal Dutch Shell in 1912. The interests were later nationalized by the Bolsheviks (section on nationalization).

The Baku Oil Society

The Baku Oil Society, or Baku Oil Company, was possibly the world's first vertically integrated oil company. It was formed in 1874 by Vasili Kokorev and Pyotr Gubonin, two prominent winners in the oil lease auctions of 1872. At around the same time, Standard Oil in the United States was integrating both horizontally and vertically, but not yet completely into upstream operations; it was mostly a refiner and marketer.

The Baku Oil Society's Antecedent was the Trans-Caspian Trade Partnership, in which Kokorev and Gubonin were also principal shareholders. The Trans-Caspian Trade Partnership, founded in 1865, established and ran a refinery at Surakhani. After the 1872 auctions, Kokorev and Gubonin deliberately set out to form a joint stock company that would cover the full spectrum of oil operations from exploration and production to refining and marketing. The initial capitalization of the new company was 2.5 million rubles.

The Baku Oil Society had oil leases in the Balakhani area and elsewhere acquired by the Trans-Caspian Trade Partnership, as well as the refinery and a fleet of schooners and barges. It had marketing outlets in Baku, Moscow, Saratov, Samara, Tsaritsyn, Nizhni Novogorod, Astrakhan, and a number of other cities. By 1876 the Baku Oil Society accounted for more than 32 percent of Russia's oil production and was the country's leading oil company. In 1879 it completed a kerosene pipeline from the Surakhani refinery to the Zykh wharf on the Caspian Sea. It also commissioned an oil tanker, *Surakhani*, from the Swedish Abo shipyard.

Beginning in 1879 the Baku Oil Society began to face formidable competition, first from Branobel and later from the Rothschilds, as well as other companies. Gradually, it lost its leadership position, despite continuing to increase its oil production. In the early 1900s, the Baku Oil Society tried to recapture its leadership of the Russian oil industry, but without success. On June 1, 1918, all its assets were nationalized by the Bolsheviks.

The Tagiyev Company

Zeinalabdin Tagiyev, born in 1823, began life as a stonemason, apprenticed to a bricklayer at the age of ten. He gradually became a successful building contractor with diversified business interests, including small-scale oil refining. In the auctions of December 1872, he partnered with an Armenian, Sarkissov, to purchase the lease on an oil property. The property, in Bibi-Eibat, was considered one of the less promising ones at the auction, and for more than a decade, it produced only small amounts of oil with considerable difficulty. Sarkissov eventually gave up and sold his interest to Tagiyev.

On September 27, 1878, Tagiyev struck a gusher that completely drenched the surrounding area. It blew for fifteen days and wasted an estimated 1.4 million barrels of oil. Tagiyev proceeded to build a refinery for what turned out to be very high-quality oil. He also built a dock and acquired a fleet of tankers for the Caspian and barges for the Volga to transport his products. He joined forces with his competitors, the Nobel brothers, to help build the Baku-Batum kerosene pipeline (see chapter 7).

Tagiyev sold his oil company for 5 million rubles in gold in 1897 to British industrialists J. Vishaw, E. Hubbard, and others, who organized the Russian Oil Petroleum and Liquid Fuel Company. Tagiyev retained 1.6 million rubles, or £165,000, worth of shares in the new company. He continued to profit from the oil industry, but he also had a vision of diversifying Azerbaijan's economy so that the region would not forever remain just a source of oil for the Russian Empire. He invested significant capital in other industries, including textiles, food processing, construction, shipping, and fishing. In 1898 Tagiyev established a new joint stock company, the Caucasian Joint Stock Company for the Processing of Fibrous Substances. He also acquired all the shares of a shipping company, the simply "Caspian" company, and established an independent merchant fleet.

The Mantashev Company

Founded by Alexander Mantashev, the Mantashev Company was organized as a joint stock company in 1899 but had been doing business in the petroleum industry for several years. Mantashev began his career in cotton and banking. In the 1890s he found a niche buying up marginally successful oil wells and making them profitable. He was also known to have an uncanny ability to choose successful drilling sites. Mantashev had a refinery in Baku to produce kerosene and a canister manufacturing factory in Batum, among many other interests. He helped fund the Baku-Batum Pipeline. Mantashev was also a significant shareholder in several petroleum companies, including Branobel.

Nationalization

After the 1917 Russian Revolution, the oil industry in Azerbaijan was nationalized. The Soviet Union was formally constituted in 1922, but various Soviet Socialist Republics existed before that date. In March 1918, all power in Azerbaijan passed into the hands of the workers, peasants, and the Baku Council of People's Commissars. The council issued a decree on June 2, 1918, declaring the oil industry the property of the people. The government of the Russian Soviet Federative Socialist Republic (RSFSR) approved the action, and on June 20, 1918, Vladimir Lenin signed a decree of the Council of People's Commissars of the RSFSR nationalizing the oil industry in Russia (CLOWPG 1918).

On April 28, 1920, the Eleventh Red Army of Soviet Russia entered Baku. This began seventy years of Soviet rule in Azerbaijan. On May 24, 1920, the Azerbaijan Revolutionary Committee issued a decree formally nationalizing the oil industry in Azerbaijan. Two hundred seventy-two private oil industrial entities, including all the ones discussed in the preceding sections of this chapter, were abolished or nationalized (Balayev 1969, 109–110).

Chapter 7

Technology and Operations

FINDING OIL: DECIDING WHERE TO DRILL

Finding oil in the nineteenth century was often a haphazard process, guided largely by the presence of surface seeps. It also relied on dubious methods such as the use of divining rods or the employment of people who could claim to sniff oil or charlatans who claimed special spiritual powers (Williamson and Daum 1959, 910). Gradually, more scientific methods were applied.

Petroleum geology as a rigorous discipline did not develop until the twentieth century, but there were many stirrings and precursors in the nineteenth. The systematic geological approach was often met with skepticism in the industry. Geologist Israel White (1892, 193) alluded to this:

> As is well known, it was formerly a popular saying among practical oil men that "Geology has never filled an oil tank;" and to such a low estate had oil geology fallen that a prominent producer of oil and gas, disgusted with geology and geologists, was once heard to remark that if he wanted to make sure of a dry hole he would employ a geologist to select the location.

Still, there was progress: the beginnings of the anticlinal theory were formulated, and the theory was successfully applied by White, as we discuss later. There was also considerable progress in understanding reservoir rocks, and some of the basic notions of a stratigraphic trap were developed. Frehner (2011) provides a useful account of nineteenth-century petroleum geology.

The Sands of Pennsylvania

In something of an accident of history, the earliest oil regions in Pennsylvania were areas where oil was not structurally, but rather stratigraphically, trapped (Sherrill, Dickey, and Matteson 1941). Stratigraphic traps can be more difficult to discern geologically than structural traps such as anticlinal ones, and for a time this influenced the course of petroleum geology in the 1860s and '70s.

Practitioners and scientists in nineteenth-century Pennsylvania Oil Regions may not have been full-fledged petroleum geologists or engineers in the modern sense, but they did have some understanding of reservoir rocks and the geology of the producing sandstones of their areas. In the earliest oil region of Venango County, drillers gave producing formations the names "First Sand," "Second Sand," and "Third Sand," as noted by J.P. Lesley's transmission letter for John F. Carll's 1880 report for the Geological Survey of Pennsylvania (1880, viii III). The sands were collectively termed the Venango Group of oil sands by various investigators, including Ashburner (1880); Carll (1880).

As noted by Dickey (1941, 8), the Venango Group is about 330 feet thick in the area of the Titusville Quadrangle and lies below the Riceville Shale. Dickey notes that the ordinally named sands can be correlated to various formally named rocks: the First Sand to the Woodcock Sandstone of Crawford County, the Second Sand to the Salamanca Sandstone of the Bradford District, and the Third Sand to the Panama Conglomerate. In other oil-producing districts, the same names might or might not mean different things. For example, "First Sand" meant essentially the same thing in the Titusville and Tidioute Quadrangles, but the "Second Sand" in Tidioute was "Red Valley Sand" in Titusville, and the "Third Sand" in Titusville was the "Fourth Sand" in Tidioute (Dickey 1941, 8). And, as we saw in chapter 5, the Bradford Third Sand did not correlate at all with the Venango Third Sand, for which it was initially named.

John Franklin Carll

Geologist and engineer John Franklin Carll (Harper 2001) was one of the first people, if not the first, to articulate the stratigraphic trapping of oil. He conducted exhaustive surveys of rock strata in Pennsylvania's oil-producing areas and gathered extensive well records. This latter activity was essential but very difficult, as many drillers kept poor records. They were interested in quick profits, not advancing the science of petroleum geology. Carll was eventually able to produce subsurface contour maps of oil-bearing strata, notably the Venango Third Sand (Carll 1874). Carll's maps clearly showed oil being trapped in stratigraphic units, without structural units such as anticlines playing a role. This probably explains Carll's famous lack of enthusiasm for the anticlinal theory.

"Oil Belt" Concept

One early idea was that of an "oil belt," a quasi-linear "vein" of oil or oil-bearing rocks extending across a large producing region. The concept, an early type of stratigraphic correlation and interpolation between producing wells, may have originated as an analogy with continuous seams of coal. It was most notably developed and applied by Cyrus Angell beginning in 1871, possibly after hearing about the idea from his associate Frederick Prentice. Angell's belt theory played a role in opening up the Lower Oil Region of Butler, Armstrong, and Clarion Counties in Pennsylvania.

Angell had three producing wells at Belle Island on the Allegheny River, south of Franklin. He noted the depths of his wells, the thicknesses of various sandstone beds, their properties, and the presence and quality of oil. He then researched other nearby wells for similar information. He found that wells at Foster Station, about nine miles away, were very similar to his own and postulated that there was some kind of oil belt between them. He and Prentice purchased or leased the land along this hypothetical belt, six miles long and thirty yards wide. Drilling in his belt, he had a 90 percent success rate. Angell proposed a second belt southwestward from Venango County into what became the Lower Oil Region. The second belt was not as predictive or productive as the first, but it was explored by many operators and did have some success.

Richard Jennings of the Armstrong Run Oil Company performed surveys and collected data in a manner similar to Angell and successfully formulated a new oil belt, the Armstrong-Butler Cross Belt that intersected Angell's. The Armstrong-Butler Cross Belt was for the "Fourth Sand," about seventy-five feet below the Third Sand. Jennings struck oil with his first well in the new belt.

Although the "oil belt" concept had some success, it was often applied haphazardly and without regard to geological fundamentals. Some operators deluded themselves into seeing "belts" where none really existed; there was also a bit too much weight placed on the idea that a "belt" should approximate a straight line and a tendency to extend that line over too great a distance. As Henry Wrigley of the Pennsylvania Geological Survey put it, "[N]ature never works with absolutely straight lines, and . . . beds of sand-rock are deposited at intervals only, as may be seen to a greater or less extent in the bottom of any running stream" (Wrigley 1874, J7).

The Anticlinal Theory

Importance of Anticlines

An anticline is a geological structure comprising folded rock strata, with the oldest beds in its interior. If it has not undergone drastic subsequent transformations altering its orientation, eroding it away, or burying it, it can coincide with a visible topographic uplift in the ground. If a permeable stratum such as a sandstone is overlain by an impermeable one such as a shale and the strata are upfolded, the conditions may exist for oil to migrate upward through the permeable stratum until it reaches the top of the fold and is blocked by the impermeable. Gas and water often accompany the oil, with gas settling in a top layer under the peak of the anticline, underlain by a layer of oil, in turn underlain by water, as dictated by the respective densities. Of the world's 998 giant hydrocarbon accumulations known in 2021, 484 involve anticlinal traps (Horn 2021).

Anticlines in the Nineteenth-Century Giants

Anticlines were even more dominant among the nineteenth-century giants. A glance at table 1.1 reveals that nine of the eleven giant oil fields discovered in the nineteenth century involved anticlinal traps, including all the American and Azerbaijani giants. This does not mean that those oil fields were explored explicitly as anticlines; they were not. The anticlinal theory was still evolving and was not yet used systematically in exploration.

Beginnings of the Theory

A number of individuals across the globe noticed the frequent coincidence of oil occurrences with topographic uplifts and anticlinal folded strata; we do not list all of them here, but Owen (1975, chapter 4) provides a good account. Thomas Oldham, an Anglo-Irish geologist, made the observation in Burma, in association with the Yenangyuang field, which was then being exploited via hand-dug wells. Ebenezer Baldwin Andrews published a similar observation in relation to the oil fields of western Virginia (Andrews 1861) and became known as the "father of the anticlinal theory," although he incorrectly theorized that oil was confined to fissures (Brice 2011). Geologist Thomas Sterry Hunt noticed the pattern in the Canadian oil region of Eniskillen, Western Ontario, and published a more complete anticlinal theory (Hunt 1862; Sorenson 2016).

In Azerbaijan, the geologist Hermann W. Abich, who made extensive studies of the geology of the Caucasus, examined the petroliferous regions of the Absheron peninsula. He correlated the distribution of mud volcanoes—in turn correlated with petroleum occurrence in the area—with anticlines (Abich 1864; Alizadeh et al. 2016, 2017; Milanovsy 2007). US geologist S.F. Emmons visited the Baku oil fields and published cross sections of the Balakhani area showing anticlinal trapping (Emmons 1898; Sorenson 2014). A.M. Konschin in 1892 identified the anticlinal structure of the Grozny oil field, visible as a topographic ridge (Owen 1975, 262). The Grozny oil field, an important early Russian field outside Azerbaijan, long exploited by hand-dug wells, was drilled in 1893. The distinguished Russian geologist Dmitri Golubyatnikov performed his work on the Absheron peninsula soon after the turn of the century, identifying the anticlinal structure of Bibi-Eibat (Thompson 1908, 109) and correctly predicting large quantities of oil in Surakhani.

Israel White and the Anticlinal Theory in Practice

As noted earlier, anticlinal notions developed over time in the nineteenth century but were not used in a major and systematic way to find oil fields, including the giant anticlinal oil fields. This situation changed with the work of geologist Israel Charles White. White applied the anticlinal theory in Pennsylvania and West Virginia to select successful drilling sites in the 1880s. His successes included the Washington, Grapeville, Belle Vernon, and Taylortown fields in Pennsylvania and, most notably, the 1888 Mannington Field in West Virginia. Mannington became one of West Virginia's most prolific fields, with the largest well producing 1,600 barrels per day (WVGES 2004). White's achievement was all the more impressive because the discovery was on a tract that legendary oilmen Guffey and Galey had previously surrendered (Owen 1975, 5.19).

DRILLING

Although the widespread drilling of wells explicitly for oil was a nineteenth-century innovation, drilling technology itself is much older. In ancient times, it was generally motivated by the search not for petroleum but for water. Percussion drilling methods were developed in China about 2,000 years ago. Bamboo framework structures, similar to modern derricks, were employed to lift and drop a heavy chiseling tool. The nineteenth-century cable tool used by Drake and others operates on the same basic principle. The Chinese drilled wells as deep as 3,000 feet, although completion may have taken several generations. At Pechelbronn (Alsace, France), as many as 140 manual wells were drilled in 1813 at an early oil-sands mining operation that had been operating since the eighteenth century. The wells were not drilled to obtain oil directly but rather to guide the development of oil-sand mining.

In the nineteenth-century United States, the development of drilling technology was driven by the search for salt. In chapter 4 we mentioned the 1808 Ruffner salt well. The Ruffners drilled their well using a rudimentary manual percussion drill powered by a spring pole. This consisted of a long timber pole, anchored at one end and propped on a fulcrum. A rope holding heavy chisel-type drilling tools was suspended from the free end of the pole. An operator would use stirrups to mount the pole and push it down with his legs so that the drill bit would hit the target. The spring pole would bring the tools back up, so a new stroke could be started. The Ruffners ushered in a vigorous salt well industry that inspired the petroleum industry.

In the 1830s through the 1850s, in what is now West Virginia, salt and drilling operations were sometimes water powered. One known instance of this, George Lemon's well, was mentioned in chapter 4. As also observed in chapter 4, Edwin Drake traveled to Tarentum, Pennsylvania, to observe salt drilling techniques. He also tapped the salt industry for an experienced driller, William A. "Uncle Billy" Smith, to act as a rig mechanic and blacksmith.

Drake's cable tool was descended from the spring-pole technique and the methods of ancient China. A wooden derrick, "Drake's yoke," about thirty feet tall, supported the tools. The steel bit, chisel-pointed and about four feet long, was suspended from rope ("cable") and was raised and dropped repeatedly to pulverize the rock. The raising of the bit was accomplished by rocking a "walking beam," driven by a steam engine. Every three to eight feet drilled, the bit was raised and a bailer lowered into the hole to remove debris. Drake also employed casing in the hole, to guard against flooding by groundwater and to keep the sides of the well from collapsing.

Cable tools, similar in concept to Drake's, continued to dominate throughout the nineteenth century and are still used in some applications today. The "Pennsylvania"-type rig had a wooden derrick, eventually standardized at 72 feet or 82 feet in height. By the early twentieth century, cable-tool rigs were more often of a kind used in California. The "California"-type had iron and steel derricks supporting heavier tools for deeper drilling. Pennsylvania-type rigs could drill to about 2,000 feet, whereas California-type rigs could drill down to 10,000 feet. Cable-tool rigs were effective and relatively simple to operate, but they were slow. They averaged about 25 feet per day, depending on the type of rock. In Azerbaijan, the first drilled productive well (not counting the 1846 well) was in 1872, using a horse-powered cable tool to a depth of 148 feet. The first steam engines appeared in Baku's oil fields in 1873. Within ten years they completely replaced animal power.

Rotary drilling technology, which is generally superior to percussion methods, was not widely used in the early oil industry and did not become dominant until the twentieth century. However, the basic ideas behind rotary drilling had a pedigree dating back to ancient Egypt. In 1844 Robert Beard obtained a US patent for a rotary drilling system with hollow drilling rods and circulating fluid to remove the cuttings. The idea underwent many improvements during the nineteenth century, and a rotary tool was indeed used in Corsicana, Texas, in 1894. One was also employed by Anthony Lucas at Spindletop in 1901. In Russia, rotary drilling with flushing was first used not in Azerbaijan but in Grozny to drill a well 1,130 feet deep.

There are a number of reasons why rotary drilling would eventually supplant cable-tool percussion drilling. Rotary rigs eliminated the laborious bailing process and could drill faster and deeper. Rotary rigs can drill hundreds or even thousands of feet per day. Initially, rotary rigs could only be used in soft rock formations. This problem was solved by the invention of the roller cone drill bit by Howard Hughes Sr. in 1908. The bit used 166 cutting edges distributed over the surfaces of two opposingly mounted metal cones. The bit ground the rock rather than chipping or scraping it and could be used in hard formations.

TORPEDOING: ANTECEDENT OF FRACKING

In the twenty-first century, horizontal drilling and hydraulic fracturing ("fracking") has been a major development in the oil industry, particularly in the United States. Fracking can make it possible to produce oil and gas that would be otherwise inaccessible because it is trapped in low-permeability formations and unable to flow satisfactorily. The application of fracking technology, along with horizontal drilling, particularly to shale formations, has enabled huge increases in the production of oil and gas in the years since 2007 in the United States and dramatically reversed, at least temporarily, the long decline in American hydrocarbon production (Vassiliou 2018).

The basic concept of fracking has roots in the oilfield technology of the nineteenth century. By detonating controlled explosions in oil wells, drillers found that they could stimulate production, or renew fading production. People had long used gunpowder to stimulate water wells, and in the 1860s the technique was also being used in oil wells, sometimes successfully, and sometimes dangerously. The technique was tamed and standardized by Edward A.L. Roberts, who had been a colonel in the Union Army during the Civil War. Roberts received patents in 1865 and 1866 for what became the "Roberts Torpedo," an explosive device detonated downhole under a column of water. Filling the hole with water was a crucial part of the technique; the water served to tamp the explosion and concentrate its beneficial fracturing effects on rock. Roberts said he got the idea of using water by observing the effects of Confederate artillery rounds hitting a narrow canal during the Battle of Fredericksburg (Wells and Wells 2021b).

Roberts's technique was effective, but his patents were controversial, given the prior use of downhole explosives to stimulate production. The controversy was magnified by the high prices he charged: $100–$200 per torpedo in money of the day and a royalty of one-fifteenth of the increased flow of oil. His ruthless zeal in enforcing his patents also caused considerable resentment. After Roberts died in 1881, his heirs sold his company to its employees, who renamed it from the Roberts Petroleum Torpedo Company to the Independent Explosives Company. The technique became widespread. In 1897 Oklahoma's first successful oil well, Nellie Johnstone No.1 (see chapter 5) was torpedoed, turning it into a gusher (Wells and Wells 2021b).

REFINING

Refining refers to the set of processes for extracting useful products from crude oil, including various types of fuel, lubricating oil, raw materials for petrochemicals, and other products. Refining in the nineteenth century focused on distilling crude oil to obtain kerosene for illumination applications.

Refining was not invented in the nineteenth century; in various forms, it has a much longer history. As Sorkhabi (2005, 170) points out, Muslim alchemists began distilling petroleum over a thousand years ago. The Persian alchemist Abu Bakr Muhammad ibn Zakariya Räzi (also known as Rhases) designed an apparatus to distill light petroleum. The apparatus is called an "alembic," from the Arabic *al-anbiq*, in turn derived from the Greek *ambix*. Much later, in 1728, chemist Jean Theophilus Hoeffel distilled crude oil from a spring in Alsace and possibly used the distillate for illumination. In Russia, the Dubinin brothers operated a refinery in 1823 in the Mozdok region of the northern Caucasus, near the village of Akki-Yurt (Matveichuk 2004, 18). There was also one in 1824 on the Taman Peninsula, probably modeled on that of the Dubinin brothers. That plant operated for a year and a half, with the finished product sold in Moscow and Kharkov. There were a number of other examples (see, for example, Brice 2008).

Silliman's Report, 1855

Benjamin Silliman Jr.'s famous report of 1855, mentioned in chapter 4's discussion of the history leading up to the Drake well, was an important event in the history of refining, because it scientifically established the various fractions comprising crude oil. By applying the technique of fractional distillation, pioneered in the United States by his father, Benjamin Silliman Sr., he recovered eight fractions, plus a residue, from a sample of Venango County, Pennsylvania, crude oil. He described these as "Product No. 1" through "Product No. 8," the latter boiling in the range from 220 to 240 degrees Centigrade, and the former being mostly water.

Silliman described the fractions qualitatively—for example, "The last product had the color and consistency of honey, and the odor was less penetrating than that of the preceding oils" (Silliman 1855, 8). He determined the densities of the fractions, ranging from 0.733 grams per cubic centimeter for

"Product No. 2" to 0.854 for "Product No. 8." Silliman's "Products" 3–6 correspond roughly to fractions we would classify today as heavy naphtha, while 7 and 8 correspond roughly to what we would classify as kerosene (based on boiling ranges tabulated in Speight 2017, 144)

Samuel Kier's Refinery, 1851

Samuel Kier distilled crude oil to produce kerosene, or something close to it, and was selling it by 1851, as discussed in more detail in chapter 5. This may have been the first refinery in the United States to produce kerosene by distillation of conventional liquid crude oil (Brice 2008). Kier also found it desirable to perform two distillations, one to produce raw kerosene and another to refine the kerosene (Mann 2009, 53).

Early Industrial Refining in Azerbaijan, 1834–1863

As mentioned in chapter 6, Nikolai Voskoboinikov designed, constructed, and tested a refinery in the Balakhani area of the Absheron peninsula in 1834, to obtain illuminating oil from Absheron crudes. The refinery was innovative and used local natural gas as a heat source. The burner was made from iron pipes with holes in them. This was probably the first industrial use of natural gas in Russia. The receiving vessel was an iron cylinder immersed in an iron vat filled with water. Voskoboinikov distilled both heavy ("black") Balakhani oil and light ("white") Surakhani oil. The Surakhani oil yielded 83.9 percent of a distillate suitable for illumination, 12.5 percent heavy residue, and 3.6 percent evaporation loss. The Balakhani oil yielded 10, 85, and 5 percent of the same, respectively (Matveichuk 2004, 20). Between November 1837 and August 1838, the refinery produced over 900 poods (~118 barrels) of illuminating oil, shipped to Astrakhan. Unfortunately, the process did not include a secondary refining step for the kerosene-like illuminating oil, which was sour and corroded the walls of the iron barrels in which it was stored—thereby itself becoming contaminated and less effective as an illuminant. Voskoboinikov was not available to continue overseeing the process and perfecting it, because he was suspended from duty in 1838 as a result of unjust accusations from which he was exonerated later that year. The refinery ceased operation in early 1839.

The first truly commercial refinery in Azerbaijan was not constructed until 1859, fifteen years after Voskoboinikov left Azerbaijan and the petroleum industry. That project was executed by V.A. Kokorev and P.I. Gubonin, who would become major players in the industry after the reforms of 1872 (chapter 6). They built the refinery in Surakhani, near the fire-worshipping temple. Initially, they used resinous shale as a feedstock, with poor results.

They obtained better illuminating oils in larger quantities by switching to crude oil. Kokorev and Gubonin were aided by Justus von Liebig, a famous German chemist, who sent his assistant E. Moldenhauer to Baku to work on the project. With Liebig's help, the "Trans-Caucasian Trade Association" imported the necessary equipment from Germany, including spherical boilers with a capacity of 100 poods (~12 barrels) for rerunning of distillate and cast iron retorts for destructive distillation.

In December 1863 Javad Melikov constructed a kerosene plant in the city of Baku and used cooling stations in the refining process for the first time. As the industry developed, he could not survive competition with larger enterprises and died in poverty. V.I. Ragozin, a prominent Russian oilman, characterized J. Melikov as follows:

> As usual with everyone who has such an idea, he saw how to realize an idea in [a new] enterprise. He was seen as a strange and eccentric man by the residents of Baku. Of course, they thought this because he did not seek financial gain and gave all he had, down to the last kopeck. He was driven purely by his desire to attain his goal. In the history of development of technical enterprises, we often face at times awkward people who are the impetus for our production by driving it ahead, but remain themselves without any business [success], dying in poverty and oblivion. Yet those who did not believe in such persons and mocked them benefited from the wealth gained on the basis of their achievements (Mir-Babayev 2008, 30).

Continuous Distillation

Refineries in the 1860s and '70s employed discontinuous distillation. Crude oil was heated in a vessel, generating vapors as well as a kerosene fraction, and leaving behind a heavy residual. The kerosene was typically redistilled to control the flash point of the final product and make it safer to use in lamps. The heavy residual could be redistilled under vacuum to obtain substances such as lubricating oils, greases, and waxes. The process was inefficient. Crude oil had to be loaded, residue had to be emptied, and frequent cleaning was required. Some refineries began using two separate distillation units, one for the distillation of the crude and another for refining the kerosene. This presaged the process of continuous distillation (Larraz 2021).

In the continuous distillation process, a series of vessels were connected to one another, and heated separately to successively higher temperatures. Material flowed by gravity from each vessel to its successor. The final vessel was heated to very high temperatures to induce cracking and improve kerosene yields. The last residue was used to obtain lubricants and fuel oil (Larraz 2021, 131–132).

Continuous Distillation in the United States

An important American innovator in the area of continuous distillation was Samuel Van Syckel, who was also noted for his early contributions in pipelines (see section on pipelines in the United States). He began experimenting in 1862, when he owned and operated a refinery in Jersey City, New Jersey. Persevering through business difficulties and fires, he perfected his process by the early 1870s and received a patent in 1877. His basic setup consisted of three connected stills, preceded by a crude oil feed tank. To oversimplify greatly: the first still removed gasoline and light fractions; the second was for kerosene; and the final one was for lubricants and heavy fuel oil. In a variation, he added a fourth still for cracking. Van Syckel promoted his process but did not succeed in generating substantial interest. This may have been because of crude oil and refining capacity surpluses in the United States at the time (Williamson and Daum 1959, 270–271).

Continuous Distillation in Azerbaijan

Dmitri Mendeleev was an innovator in this area. He first outlined a process in his notebooks on July 29, 1881. He experimented with the process that year at a refinery in Konstantinovo owned by the oilman V.I. Ragozin. He was able to produce a highly refined and clean-burning kerosene. Mendeleev also experimented at a refinery outside Moscow owned by P.I. Gubonin. He wrote:

> Large-scale experiments which I conducted at the Kuskovo refinery owned by Mr. Gubonin's partnership, Russo-American Oil Production, have shown that a non-continuous still containing 100 poods [~12 barrels] of petroleum processed an average of 150 poods [~19 barrels of kerosene] in 24 hours, if the kerosene and intermediate products were run off. When the still was redesigned and turned into a continuous one, its [24-hour] yield was at least 800 poods [~103 barrels] of refined oil (instead of 150 poods [~19 barrels]). Thus, continuous distillation means an obvious economy in building refineries and repairing stills. Once it is introduced, distilling two-thirds of the crude oil, instead of one-third at present, will not require an increase in the number of operating stills (Matveichuk 2004, 103).

As discussed in chapter 6, Ludvig Nobel developed a continuous distillation process based on some of Mendeleev's ideas (Russian Patent No. 9206, December 17, 1882). In the period from 1881 to 1884, the Nobel brothers began applying the process on a large scale to produce high-quality kerosene very efficiently by the standards of the time. By the 1890s the technology was also adopted by the Rothschild and Mantashev companies.

The Frasch Process

Chemist Herman Frasch, a German immigrant to the United States, developed a process for reducing the sulfur content of "sour" (high-sulfur) petroleum. This was an extremely important achievement, as a high sulfur content makes petroleum difficult to refine and can also degrade the ultimate products. Kerosene refined from sour oil produced foul odors when burned for illumination. The Frasch process solved this problem, increasing the range of crude oils from which kerosene could be produced and effectively marketed. Frasch sold the process to Canada's Imperial Oil Company in 1882.

As discussed in chapter 5, Standard Oil became interested in Frasch's process when it acquired massive amounts of sour Lima-Indiana oil in Ohio and Indiana. Standard bought the process and hired Frasch as a consultant, putting him in charge of what was one of the first systematic scientific research programs in the petroleum industry. Frasch's process entailed treating crude oil with metallic oxides to precipitate the sulfur. He obtained a series of patents, culminating in No. 448,480, issued in 1891, which narrowed the set of oxides to copper and lead, among other things (Scherer 2011, 231).

Vladimir Shukhov's Cracking Process

As the world moved into the twentieth century, gasoline became more important than kerosene, and increasing gasoline yields in refining was paramount. It is worth noting that Vladimir Shukhov designed a thermal cracking process to break larger molecules down into smaller ones and thus increase the proportion of light fractions (such as gasoline) recovered in refining. Shukhov devised his process with the help of his associate Sergei Gavrilov. He also built a plant to implement it. The Shukhov process was patented on November 27, 1891 (Russian Patent No. 12926), more than two decades before William Burton's thermal cracking process in the United States. Shukhov's patent was later used in US litigation by companies trying to invalidate the Burton patent. However, it should be noted that Burton's process was the one that first achieved large-scale practical application to produce increased yields of gasoline from petroleum.

TRANSPORTING OIL AND PRODUCTS

The Transport Bottleneck

In the earliest years, one of the crucial problems facing the industry in both Pennsylvania and Azerbaijan was how to transport crude oil and products to market. In 1860s Pennsylvania, oil was stored in barrels and transported in animal-drawn wagons for twenty to forty miles before reaching a railhead or a river. Illumination was not the only use for oil; some of it was used for lubrication, and some was burned as fuel. During the winter months, when demand for oil as fuel was high, the Allegheny River was essentially closed for navigation to Pittsburgh. Oil Creek was at a high enough level for oil barges for only half the year. Transportation by wagon was also slow and unreliable. Wagons typically held five to seven barrels each and regularly became stuck in mud or were stymied by snow and ice. By the mid-1860s, it cost $1.25 a barrel to transport oil to the railhead nearest to Titusville, while the total price for a barrel of crude varied roughly between $2.50 and $4.00 (BP 2020; table D.6). Meanwhile, the cost of the wooden barrel itself was at least $2.00 and often considerably higher. Barrels were used not just for transport, but also for storage, in the absence of large tanks at the wellhead.

In Azerbaijan, the situation was even direr. Peasants transported oil to refineries in Baku in whatever containers and by whatever means they could find. They used wineskins, and sometimes wooden barrels, which were in very short supply because of the relative lack of trees from which to produce lumber in the region. Containers were transported using ox-drawn carts. Miesner and Leffler (2006, 20) estimate that in the 1880s, some 10,000 peasants were involved in the transport of oil from Balakhani to Baku.

Rail Transport of US Petroleum and Products

The United States already had 30,000 miles of rail lines by 1860 (Williamson and Daum 1959, 83), although the Pennsylvania Oil Regions themselves were underserved. Still, if the oil or product could be delivered to a railhead, railroad transport was an effective way to move it over relatively long distances. This was particularly true once tank cars had been developed to transport the oil in bulk rather than in barrels.

An early attempt to transport oil in bulk by rail was the "rotary oil car" of the Pennsylvania Railroad between Pittsburgh and Philadelphia, introduced in 1865. The car consisted of two sixty-inch solid iron wheels connected by hollow axles with a capacity of about twelve barrels' worth of oil (Williamson and Daum 1959, 181). In that same year, oil producer and buyer Amos Densmore and his brother James experimented with two wooden tanks, each with a capacity of forty to forty-five barrels of oil, on a flatcar of the Atlantic and Great Western Railroad. The Densmores successfully shipped the oil from the Pennsylvania Oil Regions to New York in September 1865. On April 10, 1865, the Densmores received a US patent (No. 53,794) for an "Improved Car for Transporting Petroleum" (White 1993, 366). The Densmore car was imitated and very soon supplanted by cars with horizontal iron and steel tanks (White 1993, 367–376).

John D. Rockefeller recognized the importance of tank cars. In 1878 he established the Tank Car Trust to buy tank cars for his Union Tank Line, which he had acquired five years earlier. In 1888 Rockefeller's Standard Oil owned or controlled 5,600 of the nation's 6,100 tank cars. By the end of the century, there were roughly 13,000 tank cars in the country, and Standard Oil either owned or controlled roughly 90 percent of them (White 1993, 379).

Rail Transport of Azerbaijan Petroleum and Products

In the later nineteenth century, there were two main rail routes for transporting Baku petroleum products to market. One was via the 547-mile Trans-Caucasian Railway between Baku and Batum (renamed Batumi in 1936), on the Black Sea coast of Georgia, from where water transportation was possible to the rest of the world through the Bosporus. The Trans-Caucasian Railway began operation in 1883. The other route was via the Vladikavkaz Railway from Petrovsk to Novorossiysk on the Black Sea coast of Russia. That railway was built in stages. The earliest leg, a 434-mile main line from Rostov to Vladikavkaz, began operation in 1872.

The Novorossiysk route was preceded by water transport on the Caspian between Baku and Petrovsk. Unlike the direct route from Baku to the Black Sea offered by the Trans-Caucasian Railway, the Novorossiysk route required cumbersome offloading from Caspian tankers to railway tank cars (Oliphant 1901, 195). However, because of excise allowances for shippers to Novorossiysk and other factors, the less direct route remained competitive. In the 1890s roughly 600,000 barrels of kerosene per month could be shipped via the Trans-Caucasian Railway, while about 240,000 barrels could go via Caspian and rail to Novorossiysk. In 1898 the Vladikavkaz Railway was extended from Petrovsk to Baku (Westwood 1966, 671), so rail shipment became possible from Baku to Novorossiysk as well as to Batum. However, export volumes on the Baku-Petrovsk leg were relatively small, about twenty-three times lower than on the Trans-Caucasian Railway in 1902 (Thompson 1908, 14).

Like Standard Oil, the Nobel Brothers realized that tank cars were the most efficient way to transport oil and refined products by rail and began using them in 1881. They quickly developed a fleet of hundreds, exporting products to Europe via the railway terminals of Warsaw, Kiev, and Dvinsk and then to the rest of the world via the Trans-Caucasian and Vladikavkaz routes.

Pipelines as a More Efficient Method

Today pipelines are ubiquitous, and constitute an economical method for transporting petroleum and petroleum products over long distances. Pipeline transport today can be up to fifteen times cheaper than truck, twelve times cheaper than rail, and cheaper than barge, though on average it is somewhat more expensive than tanker. It is also less energy intensive. A typical oil pipeline might consume about 450 British thermal units per ton-mile of transport, versus 540 for barges, 680 for rail, and 2,300 for truck (these are gross averages and there can be wide variation; Vassiliou 2018).

In the early modern oil industry, pipelines were introduced in both the United States and Azerbaijan. However, pipelines predate the nineteenth-century industry. Bamboo pipes wrapped with waxed cloth were used to transport natural gas for lighting in China as early as 400 BCE. Cast iron pipes were used in the eighteenth century to transport water, sewage, and gas. The introduction of steel pipe in the nineteenth century was a major innovation, greatly increasing the strength of pipes.

Pipelines in the United States

Earliest Local Oil Pipelines in Pennsylvania

According to Williamson and Daum (1959, 183), the first person in the United States who had a definite plan to construct a pipeline for petroleum transport was Samuel Karns, who observed a well at Burning Springs, western Virginia. In 1860 he proposed to build a six-inch wooden pipeline from that well to the railhead at Parkersburg, but his plans were disrupted by the outbreak of the US Civil War; he joined the Union Army. In 1862 J.L. Hutchings constructed a 1,000-foot pipeline powered only by gravity to connect a Barrows & Company oil well on the Tarr Farm in the Oil Creek, Pennsylvania, area to the company's refinery. His second attempt at a pipeline to transport oil from the Tarr Farm over two miles to the Humboldt refinery failed. Unlike the first pipeline, the second one could not rely on gravity and required pumping over a hill. Using a rotary pump he had invented, Hutchings was able to force oil through the line. However, he was foiled by leakage at the joints where sections of pipe came together. Hutchings was able to build more successful local pipelines in the Oil Creek district in 1863 and 1864, but leakage difficulties continued to plague him. Such problems were rife in nineteenth-century pipelines and were not tamed until several technical innovations had occurred. In 1880 Solomon Dresser, who would eventually establish the company that became Dresser Industries, developed a threaded coupling with a rubber O-ring to seal the joint. Later, in the 1920s, the introduction of oxyacetylene welding and electric arc welding would make threaded joints unnecessary.

A successful product pipeline was built by the Warren refinery at Plumer, Pennsylvania, in 1864. The refinery was near Cherry Run, not far from Oil Creek. The two-inch pipeline was constructed of wrought iron and moved kerosene about three miles south to the Allegheny River. The first truly successful local-scale crude oil pipeline was built a year later by Samuel Van Syckel, connecting Pithole with a point on the Oil Creek Railroad five miles away. Van Syckel made his line out of fifteen-foot sections of two-inch wrought iron pipe. Joints between sections were lap-welded and tested to a pressure of 900 pounds per square inch. The pipeline had a throughput of nearly 2,000 barrels per day. Van Syckel even built a dedicated telegraph line for monitoring. Teamsters feared competition from the pipeline and attempted to sabotage it, but it was completed within a month of starting construction and began operating on October 10, 1865. The teamsters were right to be wary of the new pipeline: it charged a dollar per barrel for transport, one-third of the teamster rate (Williamson and Daum 1959, 185). Van Syckel's pipeline soon spurred the construction of others. By 1866 the Oil Creek region had at least seven of them, ranging in length from two to seven miles.

Expansion of Local Pipeline Network in Pennsylvania

As Pennsylvania production expanded to the Lower Oil Region of Butler, Clarion, and Armstrong Counties, the pipeline network also expanded throughout that area. By 1872 there were 2,000 miles of pipeline in the oil regions and by 1874, 4,000. One important network was the one consolidated under the aegis of the Union Pipe Line Company by 1874, with about 300 total miles of pipeline capable of moving 26,400 barrels per day.

"Benson's Folly"—the First Long-Distance Oil Pipeline

The first long-distance crude oil pipeline was built in Pennsylvania in 1879 by the Tidewater Pipeline Company, an entity created to offer oil transportation independent of Standard Oil and its railroad allies. The pipeline was an immensely difficult undertaking, and some called it "Benson's Folly," after Tidewater's president Byron D. Benson (Williamson and Daum 1959, 442).

The pipeline was six inches in diameter and 109 miles long, running from Coryville in the Bradford oil district to Williamsport. At Williamsport, oil was loaded into tank cars for transportation to New York by the Reading Railroad, which was outside Standard's orbit. This was the first pipeline that could compete directly with railroads for long-distance transport of oil, and it was constructed without the benefit of statewide eminent domain (see section on Pennsylvania legal framework), using private land transactions.

The Tidewater Pipeline was extended from Williamsport to Philadelphia in 1881 and then to Bayonne, New Jersey, near New York City in 1888. By that time, Standard Oil had acquired the refiners with which Tidewater did business, so Tidewater was forced into collaboration with Standard.

Expanding Long-Distance Pipeline Network

In 1881 Standard Oil, not wishing to be undercut, entered the long-distance pipeline arena and began constructing the National Transit Pipe Line System, two six-inch lines between Olean, New York, and Saddle River, New Jersey. As noted earlier, Standard also effectively controlled Tidewater's flow by 1888.

Independent producers from the Pennsylvania Oil Regions continued to try to circumvent Standard Oil and the railroads. In 1892 a group of them formed the United States Pipeline Company and built two 180-mile pipelines between the oil regions and the eastern Pennsylvania city of Wilkes-Barre, one for crude and one for refined products. Nevertheless, 90 percent of the investment required to construct the 6,800 miles of pipeline extant in the United States by 1900 had come from Standard Oil or the companies affiliated with it (Klass and Meinhardt 2015, 959).

In the emerging nineteenth-century oil regions of the Mid-Continent and California, the transport picture was quite different. In California there were some pipelines, but long-distance transport of oil was done by ship or rail. As for the Mid-Continent, pipelines were not constructed until the twentieth century. Independent producers in Kansas could not afford rail transport over the long distances to markets and had increasing amounts of oil languishing in tanks. Many did the only thing they could: sell out to Standard Oil.

The Pennsylvania Legal Framework

Long-distance pipelines suffered in comparison to the railroads, their main competition, because the latter enjoyed the power of eminent domain in Pennsylvania and the former did not. A good summary of the legal framework can be found in Klass and Meinhardt (2015). Pipeline companies and oil producers tried twice before 1872 to convince the Pennsylvania legislature to grant them this power as well. The powerful railroad lobby was able to block their efforts. However, the revelation of the railroads' price-fixing scheme with Standard Oil (see chapter 5) weakened the railroads' influence, at least temporarily, and in 1872 the legislature passed an eminent domain bill for pipelines.

The president of the Pennsylvania Railroad still had enough power to get the bill weakened, limiting pipeline eminent domain to eight Pennsylvania counties in the oil regions. Importantly, the grant of eminent domain excluded

Allegheny County, which contained the city of Pittsburgh and its refineries. Another limitation was that no pipeline could be constructed within five miles of the state line for the purpose of exporting oil out of the state (Klass and Meinhardt 2015, 957). The railroads managed to stymie statewide eminent domain for pipelines until 1883, well after the states of Ohio (1872) and New York (1878) had granted it.

Pipelines in Azerbaijan

Early Local Lines

The strong oil production in Balakhani during the 1870s, and the lack of transportation options, stimulated construction of a 5.6-mile crude oil pipeline to Baku in 1878, with sections of pipe imported from the United States. The pipeline was built for the Nobel Brothers by Bari, Sytenko & Co., employing the talents of Alexander Bari and Vladimir Shukhov (Mir-Babayev 2015). The pipeline had a diameter of three inches. It had a capacity of 9,600 barrels per day. In 1879 it transported 600,510 barrels (Alekperov 2011, 119). Soon after, Bari Sytenko built a kerosene pipeline for the Baku Oil Company from its refinery in Surakhani to the Zykh pier on the Caspian Sea. By 1884 the Baku oilfields had five pipelines (three connecting Balakhani with Baku, one connecting Balakhani to a refinery in Surakhani, and one from the Surakhani plant to the Zikh headland) with a total throughput capacity of nearly 24,000 barrels of oil or product per day (Mir-Babayev 2015).

The Baku-Batum Pipeline

Azerbaijan's major pipeline achievement was the 547-mile, eight-inch kerosene pipeline from Baku to Batum on the Black Sea Coast of Georgia. Although it was only completed in 1907, it had been discussed and planned for decades. Herbert Tweddle, an American engineer, was the first to propose construction of a long-distance pipeline to transport oil out of Baku. In 1877–1878, he and Konstantin Bodisko, a bureaucrat from the Russian Ministry of Finance, prepared proposals to construct pipelines from Baku to ports on the Caspian, Black and Azov seas (Mir-Babayev 2015).

After the Trans-Caucasian Railway opened in 1883, the specific idea of a pipeline paralleling the route began to take hold. A motivating force was the high cost and the difficulty of transporting products via the Trans-Caucasian Railway. Alekperov (2011, 120) reports that "out of a total of 15 million rubles earned in 1892 from the sale of Russian petroleum products, 11.2 million went to the board of the Transcaucasian Railway, while only 3.8 million rubles went to oil industrialists." The prominent oilman Zeinalabdin Tagiyev enunciated his support for the pipeline in a presentation at the Baku branch of the Imperial Russian Technical Society (IRTS) on January 11, 1886. In his report titled "How to Get Out of the Oil Industry Crisis," Tagiyev outlined a clear plan to export kerosene from Baku to Batum via pipeline. In November 1886 a group of about fifty Baku businessmen, including both Tagiyev and Emanuel Nobel, asked the minister of state properties for permission to construct their own Trans-Caucasian pipeline. However, it wasn't until 1893 that the Cabinet of Ministers made a preliminary decision to proceed, with the proviso that work should be done in conjunction with Bari's company (Mir-Babayev 2015).

One of the champions of the pipeline was the great scientist Dmitri Mendeleev, father of the periodic table. Mendeleev suggested pipelines for transporting oil as early as 1863. In 1877 he suggested a long-distance pipeline. In his fundamental work *Foundations of Chemistry* (St. Petersburg, 1895, 6th edition), Mendeleeev noted: "When an oil pipeline from Baku to the Black Sea is constructed in the South Caucasus (there are many of them in America, they deliver crude oil from Pennsylvania to the ocean coast, where oil is turned into kerosene and other products), Baku oil will without any doubt find a huge market" (Mir-Babayev 2015).

There was stiff opposition to the pipeline from individuals and organizations that were earning considerable fees—legal and otherwise—from the transport of oil via the railway. Eventually, a compromise was reached whereby the pipeline would coexist with the railroad. In 1886 Tagiyev wrote a letter to the governor of the Caucasus, Prince Alexander Mikhailovich Dondukov-Korsakov, about the urgent necessity to build a Caspian-Black Sea main pipeline. Following Tagiyev's initiative, local entrepreneurs led by Aghabala Quliyev set up a joint stock company to fund the construction. In 1888 Alphonse de Rothschild put up 1 million rubles in 4 percent domestic bonds as security, at the Crédit Lyonnais Saint Petersburg branch. He also financed design work by the engineer Vladimir Shukhov. Rothschild wrote to Saint Petersburg, "I have all grounds to hope that the work we would like to realize will bring an income on the capital invested and will promote the industrial and commercial development of the country."

As we have noted, appeals to the Russian government took a long time to bear fruit. On May 23, 1896, however, the Russian State Council finally decided definitively to build the pipeline, along the existing route of the Trans-Caucasian Railway. In summer that year, the Russian Ministry of Railroads sent Nikolay Shchukin, a professor at the Saint Petersburg Technological Institute, and engineer L. Wartenburg to the United States to learn American techniques of pipeline engineering and construction. The government ordered that sections of pipe be made in Russia, at plants in Mariupol, Sosnovitsy, and Yekaterinoslavl. Sections were built following American designs, with a V-thread tapering toward the end for a better seal. Work on the first leg of the pipeline, 141 miles long from Mikhaylovo to Batum, began in September 1896. Sections of pipe began arriving in 1898, and by June 1899, 87 miles of pipe had been laid. The entire first leg was completed by March 14, 1900. On June 12, 1901, Tsar Nicholas II approved completion of the entire pipeline. The second leg, bringing the pipeline 87 miles closer to Baku, was finished in 1904 and put in operation. The final and longest leg, to Baku, was completed in 1907 (Alekperov 2011).

The pipeline had sixteen pumping stations and a dedicated suspension bridge over the Kura River. Pumps for the stations along the first leg were imported from the United States. They were made by the Worthington Company and were powered by steam engines. Other pumps along the later legs were made in Russia and powered by diesel engines. The pipeline was protected from corrosion via the use of red lead paint. To avoid leakage problems, it had check valves installed every one or two miles along its length. Pumps would be shut off automatically if pressure dropped by 15 percent (Alekperov 2011).

The pipeline had a capacity of 20,000 barrels per day of kerosene and was the world's longest and most effective product pipeline at the time. It gave the Baku oil industry a warm-water port with access to world markets through the Bosporus. It played an instrumental role in enabling Marcus Samuel, an important supporter of the project, to break Standard Oil's near monopoly on the kerosene markets of Asia and led to the growth of Samuel's Shell Transport and Trading Company, one of the root companies of Royal Dutch Shell.

The Soviet Union would eventually add a crude oil pipeline between Baku and Batum in 1930. It is worth noting that the later 1930 pipeline incorporated a number of ideas from the 1870s developed by Russian engineer Sigismund Wojslaw. For example, it eliminated intermediate tanks at pumping stations, a source of loss of light hydrocarbons.

Seagoing Tankers

The first ship known to have carried oil over long distances was the brig *Elizabeth Watts*, which transported 224 tons from the United States to England in 1861. However, the *Elizabeth Watts* was not a specialized tanker in the modern sense. It did not carry the oil in bulk in its hull, but rather carried barrels of oil.

The area of seagoing tankers is one where Azerbaijan was a clear leader. The Nobel brothers had a fleet of early modern tankers plying the Caspian by the mid-1880s. The first modern oil tanker, the *Zoroaster*, was a steamer designed in 1877 by Ludvig Nobel with the help of Sven Almqvist, chief engineer at Motala Verkstad in Sweden. It was built in 1878 at the Motala shipyard in Norrköping and sailed to the Caspian via the Baltic Sea, the

Volga-Baltic Waterway, and the Volga River (Tolf 1976, 50–55). *Zoroaster* was 184 feet long, with a beam of 27 feet and a draft of 9 feet. It could carry 242 tons (~1,895 barrels) of kerosene across the Caspian in two large iron tanks joined by pipes. It also had twenty-one vertical cylindrical tanks for buoyancy.

The *Zoroaster* made its maiden voyage between Baku and Astrakhan in late 1878, and in October that year, Nobel ordered two more tankers of the same design: the *Buddha* and the *Nordenskjöld*. In 1880 Ludvig Nobel completed the design of a newer tanker, *Moses*, that used the hull of the vessel as the wall of a bulk cargo hold. Within a year, he ordered several more single-hulled tankers: *Mohammed*, *Tatarin*, *Bramah*, *Spinoza*, *Socrates*, *Darwin*, *Koran*, *Talmud*, and *Calmuck*. Another way in which Nobel's ships were ahead of their time is that they burned a type of fuel oil instead of coal to power their steam engines.

In 1881 the *Nordenskjöld* exploded while being loaded with kerosene in Baku, killing half the crew. This prompted Nobel to design a flexible loading pipe between the tanker and the shore. The pipe's couplings could move with the ship and remain fastened to the loading hole, reducing the risk of leaks and explosions. Another issue with early tankers was that, because they carried all their oil in a single, large hold, the oil could move around in bulk and cause dangerous imbalances in the ship. In 1883, Colonel Henry F. Swan, a British engineer then collaborating with the Nobel company, solved the problem with a multihold design. The new design was first implemented in the tankers *Blesk*, *Lumen*, and *Lux*. The several parallel holds each spanned the width of the ship, and were subdivided into port and starboard sections by a longitudinal bulkhead. Each compartment had its own expansion tank (Tolf 1976, 58).

Another important early tanker was the *Gluckauf*, a non-Nobel ship built in 1877. It was a British ship, not an American one, but its purpose was to carry American oil to Europe. It was designed by the aforementioned Henry Swan and built in 1885 at the Armstrong-Whitworth works in Newcastle upon Tyne. The 2,700-ton steamer's design owed much to Ludvig Nobel's earlier tankers. At 318 feet long, with a 37-foot beam and a 19-foot draft, it was considerably larger than the earlier *Zoroaster*. Unlike Nobel's early tankers, which plied the Caspian, the *Gluckauf* was a true oceangoing tanker. In July 1886 it delivered its first cargo of American oil at Geestemunde in Germany. The Gluckauf used large hull-integrated tanks filled and emptied by pipes leading ashore. Like Nobel's tankers, it obviated the costly need to place the oil in barrels before shipping. As in Swan's earlier designs, the oil storage tanks were separated from each other by a bulkhead along the centerline and a series of transverse bulkheads. There was a trunk above the tanks to allow for the expansion of the oil in warmer waters. A pump room lay between the tanks and the engine room, which was in the rear. On March 25, 1893, the *Gluckauf* ran aground on Fire Island in New York State.

The Americans did not lead initially in the design of tankers, but they were quick to adopt and exploit the new technology. By 1891 Standard Oil and affiliated companies had a fleet of nearly seventy coal-powered tanker steamships carrying oil in bulk between the United States, Europe, and other areas at speeds of eight to ten knots. The tankers carried 20,000–30,000 barrels of oil. After the invention of the diesel engine in 1897, tankers and other merchant ships began converting to oil power. Nobel was advanced in that area too; in 1903 the company built two oil tankers, the *Vandal* and the *Sarmat*, that ran on diesel-fueled internal combustion engines.

Conclusion

DOMINANCE OF AZERBAIJAN AND THE UNITED STATES

As we have observed, the story of the nineteenth-century oil industry was largely a story of the United States and Azerbaijan. Certainly, important early developments took place in Romania, Austro-Hungarian Galicia, Canada, and elsewhere. However, in the final analysis, 97 percent of world oil production during the nineteenth century took place in the United States and Azerbaijan. Over the course of the century, the dominant producing region within the United States was the Appalachian one, particularly the states of Pennsylvania, Ohio, and West Virginia. Pennsylvania alone accounted for 39 percent of nineteenth-century oil production in the world. As in later eras, oil production was dominated by a relatively few giant fields: Bibi-Eibat and the Balakhani complex in Azerbaijan and Bradford and Lima-Indiana in the United States. Together these four giants accounted for just over half the world's total oil production over the course of the nineteenth century.

DEVELOPMENT OF INDUSTRY AND THE ROLE OF GOVERNMENT

The industries in the United States and Azerbaijan developed along markedly different paths, driven largely by the different attitudes to private property and the role of government in the two societies. In Azerbaijan, the oil fields were the property of the Imperial Russian government, which, before 1872, either managed the fields directly or leased them out in a monopolistic fashion, suppressing competition and disallowing widespread private exploration and development. After the reforms introduced by Tsar Alexander II in 1872, the government continued to own the fields but leased out producing or promising properties on a competitive basis to more parties, including foreign ones. Private industry flourished for the remainder of the century on that basis.

In the United States, federal and state governments never owned or controlled the oil industry. Private landowners owned the rights to petroleum under their land. A myriad number of oil companies, large and small, obtained leases when necessary, in exchange for payment in some form. The industry originated in private enterprise and grew in the same manner. Suppression of competition, when it occurred, did not come from the government, but from private-sector companies that had grown large and powerful, such as Standard Oil. When the government did finally make a major incursion into the industry, it was in an attempt to restrain anticompetitive practices. The US government eventually broke up Standard Oil in the early twentieth century.

BUSINESS CONCENTRATION

As we have just mentioned, there was considerable concentration in the US oil industry after the competitive free-for-all of the 1860s and early 1870s. By 1881 Standard Oil had achieved significant horizontal integration and controlled over 90 percent of refinery capacity in the United States. Even after considerable backlash and the opening of new oil regions, it still managed to maintain over 80 percent control in the period from 1895 to 1897. After integrating vertically and acquiring huge producing properties in the Lima-Indiana field, Standard controlled a large proportion of upstream oil assets as well. By 1891 Standard held properties producing about a quarter of the US national output of crude.

In Azerbaijan, after the reforms of 1872, business concentration was lower. No one company ever achieved the dominance that Standard Oil enjoyed for a time in the United States. Leadership was shared among six companies that together accounted for nearly 48 percent of Azerbaijani oil production at the end of the century: the Nobel Brothers' company Branobel; the Baku Oil Society; the Tagiyev firm; the Mantashev firm; the Caspian and Black Sea Oil Company of the Rothschilds; and the Caspian Company. There is little evidence that these firms colluded with one another in the late nineteenth century. If anything, there was considerable enmity between them, and they competed fiercely (Marvin 1891, 219).

TECHNOLOGICAL LEADERSHIP

There was significant innovation in the nineteenth-century oil industry, and it occurred in both the United States and Azerbaijan. Moser (2018, 40) cites a number of scholarly sources arguing that Tsarist Russia was a technology laggard. While this may have been true in general, it was not true of the oil industry after 1872, as acknowledged by Moser himself. Certainly, before that date, Russia was behind the United States. Although the first industrial oil well was drilled in Baku in 1846, the industry in Azerbaijan continued to harvest oil in old ways from hand-dug wells. It was the Americans who introduced mechanized drilling, pipelines, and tank-car transport.

However, the Azerbaijani industry made early innovations in refining, with Voskoboinikov's refinery dating to the 1830s. The industry also made several later innovations, including continuous distillation independent of efforts in the United States, and a thermal cracking process that preceded the widespread American one by over two decades. The Azerbaijani industry led the world in designing and using seagoing tanker ships for oil transport. Some of those ships burned heavy fuel oil for propulsion rather than coal. Azerbaijan was thus an innovator in the use of petroleum for its ultimate major use—energy in the service of transport. Azerbaijan also made major strides in rail transport using tank cars and in long-distance pipelines, as evidenced by the 547-mile, eight-inch kerosene pipeline from Baku to Batum. Meanwhile, the great chemist Dmitri Mendeleev was a leader in establishing the scientific study of petroleum. Azerbaijan lagged behind the United States in the 1860s, but by the 1890s it had caught up and developed leadership of its own.

Appendix A

Barrels and Poods

The American oil industry has measured the quantity of oil in volumetric terms since its very beginnings. A barrel of petroleum is equivalent to 42 US gallons. Note that this is different from the accepted definitions of a barrel outside the petroleum industry. For example, a standard US barrel for liquid goods other than petroleum or its products is 31.5 US gallons, and a standard British one is 36 imperial gallons.

The standard petroleum barrel originated in the Pennsylvania oil fields in the nineteenth century. Barrels were originally forty gallons and then grew to forty-two. In a few cases, companies used a forty-three-gallon barrel standard. The common abbreviation for barrel as well as barrels is bbl, or b when used in combination with other measures, as in bpd (barrels per day). Some investigators have reported that bbl stands for "blue barrel," describing the particular barrels used by Standard Oil in the nineteenth century. However, it appears that this explanation may be apocryphal. The origin of bbl is not clear, but it was used much earlier than the beginnings of the Pennsylvania oil industry.

In the nineteenth-century Azerbaijani industry, oil and products were measured and reported in poods (alternatively, pouds or puds). The pood was an old Russian unit equivalent to 16.3805 kilograms.

Conversion from poods to barrels requires a knowledge of the density. Day (1922, 322) reports an average density for Russian oil of 0.859 grams per cubic centimeter, which results in an estimate of 8.3374 poods per barrel, or 7.32 barrels per metric ton.

Appendix B

Important Individuals

Abich, Hermann W. (1806–1886). Father of geology in the Caucasus.

Alexander II, tsar of Russia (1818–1881). Approved regulations in 1872 placing the Azerbaijani oil industry on a modern footing and stimulating explosive growth in oil production.

Bard, Thomas Robert (1841–1915). Drilled a successful early well in southern California in 1867. Cofounder of the Union Oil Company of California in 1890; president of Union Oil, 1890–1894.

Bissell, George Henry (1821–1884). Founder of the Pennsylvania Rock Oil Company, one of the world's first modern oil companies.

Carll, John Franklin (1828–1904). Pioneering petroleum geologist and engineer.

Cullinan, Joseph Steven (1860–1937). Early refiner in the Corsicana field, Texas. Founder of the Texas Company (later Texaco).

Doheny, Edward Laurence (1856–1935). Early oil entrepreneur in California and Mexico; discoverer of the Los Angeles City oil field, 1892.

Drake, Edwin Laurentine (1819–1880). Supervised drilling seminal 1859 well near Titusville, Pennsylvania, helping to launch the modern American oil industry.

Flagler, Henry Morrison (1830–1913). American entrepreneur who partnered with John D. Rockefeller to establish the Standard Oil Company in 1870.

Frasch, Herman (1851–1914). Chemist who developed a process, patented in 1887, for the removal of sulfur from oil.

Gesner, Abraham Pineo (1797–1864). Canadian geologist who developed processes for extracting high-quality illuminating oil from asphalt and coal and who coined the word "kerosene" to denote it.

Golubyatnikov, Dmitri Vasilyevich (1866–1933). A founder of petroleum geology in Azerbaijan. Identified the anticlinal structure of Bibi-Eibat and correctly predicted large quantities of oil in Surakhani.

Guffey, James McClurg (1839–1930). Oil entrepreneur; cofounder of Guffey and Galey, Guffey Petroleum, and Gulf Refining, antecedents of Gulf Oil Corporation.

Hazlett, Robert W. (1828–1899). Drilled the first successful oil well in what is today West Virginia, in 1859, roughly contemporaneous with Drake.

Hunt, Thomas Sterry (1826–1892). American chemist and mineralogist who elucidated the anticlinal theory of oil trapping in 1861.

Jones, William E. "Grumble" (1824–1864). Confederate general who led the first-known purposeful raid on an oil field, at Burning Springs (present-day West Virginia), on May 9, 1863.

Kier, Samuel Martin (1813–1874). Early marketer and refiner of Pennsylvania oil in the 1840s and '50s; one of the first to establish a market value for petroleum.

Lucas, Anthony Francis (1855–1921). Engineer and geologist who discovered oil at Spindletop on January 10, 1901.

Łukasiewicz, Ignacy (1822–1882). Early oil entrepreneur and a pioneer in refining kerosene from crude oil in Austro-Hungarian Galicia.

Mantashev, Alexander Ivanovich (1842–1911). Russian oil entrepreneur of Armenian descent; founder of the Mantashev Company in 1899.

Mendeleev, Dmitri Ivanovich (1834–1907). Russian chemist who developed the periodic table of the elements and had significant involvement in the nineteenth-century Azerbaijan oil industry.

Nobel, Emanuel (1859–1932). Head of Branobel from 1888 until 1918, when it was nationalized by the Bolsheviks. Son of Ludvig Nobel.

Nobel, Ludvig (1831–1888). Swedish entrepreneur and engineer who was a major force in creating the modern oil industry in Russia. With his brother Robert, he founded the Nobel Brothers Petroleum Production Company, or Branobel, in 1879.

Orcutt, William Warren (1869–1942). Petroleum geologist who organized the first oil company geological research department in 1900, at Union Oil.

Roberts, Edward A.L. (1829–1881). Inventor of the Roberts Torpedo, for stimulating oil production.

Rockefeller, John Davison (1839–1937). American industrialist who founded Standard Oil in 1870 with Henry Flagler. By some calculations, he became the richest American who has ever lived.

Rothschild, Alphonse de (1827–1905). Head of the Paris branch of the House of Rothschild, which owned major companies in the Azerbaijani oil industry beginning in 1883.

Samuel, Marcus (1853–1927). Founder of Shell Transport and Trading Company in 1897; later cofounder of Royal Dutch Shell. Shipped the Rothschilds' petroleum products from Russia to Asia, undercutting Standard Oil.

Scott, Thomas Alexander (1823–1881). Fourth president of the Pennsylvania Railroad (1874–1880). Organized the South Improvement Company in 1871, generally seen as a scheme by which John D. Rockefeller could expand Standard Oil's control of the oil industry.

Semyonov, Vasili Nikolayevich (1801–1863). Russian government official who helped promote the ideas of Nikolai Voskoboinikov on drilling for oil instead of hand-digging large pits; instrumental in laying the groundwork for the 1846 Baku well.

Shukhov, Vladimir Grigorievich (1853–1939). Russian engineer and architect who invented an early thermal cracking process for petroleum. He also designed pipelines, barges, storage tanks, pumps, and one of the first furnaces to process residual oil.

Silliman, Benjamin Jr. (1816–1885). American chemist who distilled and analyzed crude oil samples and reported on their potential products and uses, leading to the drilling of the Edwin Drake well near Titusville, Pennsylvania, and helping launch the modern petroleum industry in the United States.

Stewart, Lyman (1840–1923). Oil producer in southern California beginning in the 1880s. Cofounder of Union Oil Company of California in 1890.

Tagiyev, Zeinalabdin (1823–1924). Early entrepreneur in the Azerbaijani oil industry. Struck an 1878 gusher in Bibi-Eibat.

Van Syckel, Samuel (1813–1894). Built the first successful local oil pipeline, in 1865, connecting Pithole, Pennsylvania, to the Oil Creek Railroad five miles away. Invented a continuous distillation process.

Vorontsov, Grand Duke Mikhail Semyonovich (1782–1856). Russia's first viceroy of the Caucasus; authorized the funds for drilling the 1846 Baku well.

Voskoboinikov, Nikolai Ivanovich (1801–1860). Russian engineer working in the Baku area; among the first in the modern era to propose deliberate drilling for petroleum.

Washington, George (1732–1799). First president of the United States of America. Bequeathed land including a "bituminous spring" (near present-day Malden, West Virginia) to the public.

White, Israel (1848–1927). First to apply the anticlinal theory successfully to discover oil, most notably West Virginia's Mannington Field in 1888.

Williams, James Miller (1818–1890). Early oil entrepreneur in Ontario, Canada, beginning in the 1850s.

Appendix C

Chronology

6th century BCE

The army of Cyrus the Great (Cyrus II) of Persia uses Absheron oil in fire-based weapons to take castles and cities.

4th century BCE

Greek historian Plutarch (AD 50–120) notes that soldiers of Alexander the Great used Absheron oil for illumination, transporting it in wineskins or earthenware crockery.

Fire-worshipper temples in Surakhani (near Baku) and other places where oil and gas are extracted are destroyed during Alexander the Great's attack on what is now Azerbaijan.

1273

Venetian traveler Marco Polo (1254–1324) observes oil exports from Baku to countries of the Near East. He mentions a fountain of oil discharging such a great quantity that people load it on camel caravans. He notes that the oil is used as a salve to cure skin diseases in people and cattle and also for illumination.

1320

Catalan missionary monk Jordan of Severac observes oil extraction from wells in Baku.

1415–1440

Native Americans dig pits from which they collect seeping oil, in the future oil regions of northwestern Pennsylvania. They line the pits with logs cut using stone axes.

1594

Allahyar Mammedali Nur Ogli leaves a signed stone dated 1594 in a hand-dug oil well 115 feet deep in the Baku settlement of Balakhani.

1637

Baku oil is marked as a "terrible weapon of ignition" in a weapons inventory in Moscow.

1666

Dutch sailor and traveler Jan Struys notes that there are wells lined with stones producing white (light) and black (heavy) oil on Besh Barmag Mountain (now in the Siazan region of Azerbaijan).

1670

A map by the missionary René de Bréchant de Galinée shows an oil spring in Cuba, New York, designating it as "Fontaine de bitumen." This is not far from the area of the future Bradford Oil Field.

1723

Russian tsar Peter I (Peter the Great) issues special decrees on oil extraction. In a letter to Major General Michael Matyushkin, governor of Baku, he demands "one thousand poods of white oil or as much as possible, and to look for increase in production." Peter I annexes Baku and Derbent (on the East coast of the Caspian) to Russia. The territories soon revert to Persian rule.

1737

Fifty-two hand-dug wells are producing oil at the site of the present-day giant Balakhani field on the Absheron peninsula.

1748

Peter Kalm of Sweden publishes a map showing oil seeps in Oil Creek, in what is now Pennsylvania.

1771

Academician Samuel Gmelin visits Baku, describes oil production, and confirms that white oil is used for illumination in Surakhani.

1775

Don Pedro Fages observes oil pools in what is today southern California.

1781

Count Marko Voinovich, chief of a Caspian expedition, observes signs of oil and gas coming from the bottom of the Caspian Sea near the island Zhiloy (Chilov). In 1781–1782 he creates a detailed map of the eastern part of the Caspian Sea.

1790

Oil is struck near present-day Elizabeth, West Virginia, by drillers trying to find water.

1799

President George Washington dies. He leaves a hydrocarbon spring on his lands in western Virginia, to the public in his will.

1803

Haji Kasimbey Mansurbekov begins offshore oil extraction in Bibi-Eibat Bay from two wells eighteen and thirty meters away from coastline. A strong storm will destroy the wells in 1825.

1806

All oil resources of Absheron, Guba, and Salyan belonging to the Baku Khanate are requisitioned and declared state assets of Russia. There are about 120 wells in the Baku area with an annual production of 200,000 poods (~24,000 barrels) of oil. The tsar's government establishes the first monopolistic lease-out regime, which will last until 1824.

1808

David and Joseph Ruffner manually drill a fifty-eight-foot salt well near the Kanawha River, near present-day Charleston, West Virginia, and find oil.

1814

Robert McKee and Silas Thorla manually drill a well looking for salt near what is now Caldwell, Ohio, and strike oil.

1821

A natural gas well is drilled in Fredonia, New York, and some local buildings are served with gas for lighting.

1825

An order from Russian finance minister Yegor Frantsevich Kankrin places all oil wells under the direct control of the state, abolishing the first monopolistic lease-out regime that began in 1806. Direct control will last until 1826.

1826

The tsar's government establishes a second monopolistic lease-out regime, which will last through 1834.

1829

There are eighty-two oil wells in Baku, producing about 30,000 barrels over the year, as reported by Johann Lentz.

The Great American Well, manually drilled for salt in southern Kentucky, strikes a gusher of oil.

1835

The tsar's government abolishes the second monopolistic lease-out regime and takes direct control of the oil wells. Direct control will last through 1849.

1837

Nikolay Voskoboinikov's oil refinery starts to operate in Balakhani, becoming the world's first-known industrial oil refinery (the first similar factory in the United States will be constructed later, by Samuel Kier in 1851).

1840

Steamship transport of kerosene begins between Baku and Astrakhan. The kerosene is stored in metal drums, with a capacity up to twenty poods (~2.6 barrels) each.

1842

June 24: The Rathbone family manually drills for salt in Burning Springs, present-day West Virginia, and strikes oil.

1844

A report detailing ideas developed by Nikolay Voskoboinikov on drilling for oil rather than digging pits by hand is presented to the Russian government on the Absheron peninsula by Vasili Semyonov, a member of the Main Administration of the Trans-Caucasus.

1845

Grand Duke Mikhail Vorontsov, governor of the Caucasus, authorizes funds for oil drilling, following the ideas of Nikolai Voskoboinikov, as presented by Vasili Semyonov.

1846

In Bibi-Eibat (Baku) the world's first drilled industrial oil well is bored to a depth of sixty-nine feet, under the direction of Vasili Semyonov. The work is performed by Major Alexeev (director of Baku oil fields) and his team, employing the ideas of N. Voskoboinikov.

Abraham Gesner develops a distillation process yielding an illuminating oil from albertite.

1847

July 8–14: The governor general of the Caucasus, Grand Duke Mikhail Vorontsov, officially confirms completion of the world's first industrial oil well drilled in 1846 in Bibi-Eibat.

1848

Samuel Kier begins bottling oil, a by-product from his family's brine wells at Tarentum, Pennsylvania. He markets "Kier's Rock Oil" as a patent medicine.

A second well is drilled in Baku under the auspices of the Russian government.

1850

The tsar's government relinquishes direct management of the oil wells and establishes the third and final monopolistic lease-out regime, which will last until 1872.

1851

Samuel Kier refines crude oil in Pittsburgh, Pennsylvania, and begins selling the product as an illuminant.

Early 1850s

Andrés Pico collects oil from seeps in Pico Canyon, in present-day Los Angeles County, California. He distills the crude to create illuminating oil for the San Fernando Mission.

George Lemon drills for salt using water-powered machinery and strikes oil near present-day Parkersburg, West Virginia, and finds oil.

1851

Samples of Azerbaijani oil are exhibited at the International Exhibition in London, in the "Chemical products" section. The Russian delegation to the exhibition is headed by Grand Duke Mikhail Vorontsov, governor general of the Caucasus.

1854

December 30: George Bissell and Jonathan Eveleth establish the Pennsylvania Rock Oil Company of New York to produce oil from surface seeps or via hand-dug wells.

1855

Benjamin Silliman Jr. issues a report to the Pennsylvania Rock Oil Company analyzing Venango County, Pennsylvania, oil, and identifying the main fractions of crude oil.

September 18: The Pennsylvania Rock Oil Company of New York is reconstituted as the Pennsylvania Rock Oil Company of Connecticut. It later becomes the Seneca Oil Company.

1857

Charles Morrell of San Francisco produces kerosene from a small refinery in eastern Santa Barbara County, California.

1858

The Seneca Oil Company employs Edwin Drake to drill for oil in Pennsylvania.

1859

August 27: Edwin Drake strikes oil at Oil Creek, Pennsylvania, and launches the first modern oil boom. Drake uses a cable-tool drill powered by a steam engine and cases the hole.

Lewis Ross manually drills a salt well in present-day Oklahoma and strikes oil.

Robert W. Hazlett successfully drills for oil at Oil Spring Run, near the town of Petroleum in present-day West Virginia.

V.A. Kokorev, P.I. Gubonin, and German baron N.E. Tornow construct the first commercial refinery in Azerbaijan. It will begin producing kerosene in 1861.

1860

V.E. Eikhler, a Moscow University chemist, works at Kokorev's refinery under the instruction of Dmitri Mendeleev and conducts research into scientific methods of oil refining. Later, Mendeleev will name Eikhler "veteran of the Baku oil industry."

There are 218 wells on the Absheron peninsula; well construction resembles a stepped, inverted pyramid.

Ohio's first commercial oil well is manually drilled in Macksburg.

1861

April 17: Henry Rouse drills Pennsylvania's first gusher, in the Oil Creek area.

Brewer, Watson and Co. drill the McClintock No. 1 Well in the Oil Creek area. It will produce continuously for 150 years.

California's first well intentionally seeking oil is drilled on the Davis Ranch in Humboldt County, in the northern part of the state.

The brig *Elizabeth Watts* transports 224 tons of oil from the United States to England.

Ebenezer Baldwin Andrews publishes observations of anticlinal structures in relation to the oil fields of western Virginia. In the next year, Thomas Sterry Hunt will publish a more complete anticlinal theory.

1863

Javad Melikov of Baku designs and constructs an oil refinery for the production of kerosene from crude oil in Baku. Within a decade, about fifty refineries are functioning in Baku.

May 9: A Confederate Army unit led by General W.E. "Grumble" Jones raids Burning Springs, in present-day West Virginia. The Confederates set fire to oil wells and destroy infrastructure and stored oil.

1864–1865

Benjamin Silliman Jr. issues reports predicting large-scale oil deposits in southern California. They are judged too optimistic and damage his reputation, but he is proved correct in the long run.

1865

"Photonaphthil," an illumination product of the Trans-Caspian Trading Company's oil refinery at Surakhani, receives a Silver Medal at the Moscow Exhibition of Manufactured Products. The company is headed by Vasili Kokorev and Pyotr Gubonin.

The first successful local-scale crude oil pipeline is built by Samuel Van Syckel, connecting Pithole, Pennsylvania, with a point on the Oil Creek Railroad five miles away. It is constructed of two-inch wrought iron pipe.

September: James and Amos Densmore build a railroad tank car and use it to ship oil from the Pennsylvania Oil Regions to New York.

A.L. Roberts receives his first patent for what will became the "Roberts Torpedo," an explosive device detonated downhole under a column of water to stimulate production. He receives a further patent the next year.

1866

The first oil tank for storage, measurement, and supply of oil is constructed in the area of Lake Boyukshor (near Baku).

September 12: Lyne T. Barret drills the first well purposely seeking oil in Texas, in Nacogdoches County.

1867

Mechanic K. Veizer uses oil residue as a fuel for the first time in Baku: he burns it on a fire grate.

1870

John D. Rockefeller and Henry Flagler establish the Standard Oil Company in Cleveland, Ohio.

The Surakhani refinery of V. Kokorev and P. Gubonin receives an award for "preparation of lighting oils of rather high quality from Caucasian oil, by extensive manufacture at a factory," at the All-Russia manufactured goods exhibition in Saint Petersburg.

1871

Job Moses drills the discovery well of the giant Bradford Oil Field, just north of Bradford, Pennsylvania.

Cyrus Angell begins applying the "belt theory" of oil occurrence, helping to open up the "Lower Oil Region" of Butler, Armstrong, and Clarion Counties in Pennsylvania.

1872

February 1: Russian emperor Alexander II (1818–1881) issues the "Decree on oilfield development and excise from photogenic manufacture," which puts an end to the monopolistic lease-out system for the oil industry of Azerbaijan and Russia in general.

February–March: The "Cleveland Massacre"—Standard Oil buys out twenty-two of its twenty-six competitors in the Cleveland refining industry.

The oil and trading company "Haji Zeinalabdin Tagiyev" is founded.

The Pennsylvania legislature passes a limited eminent domain bill for pipelines.

December 7–28: Four weekly, highly competitive auctions of oil leases are conducted in Baku. Each lease is for a twenty-seven-acre plot. Many individuals and companies are able to obtain leases.

1873

Mass drilling of oil wells begins around Baku.

June: The first powerful oil gusher, Vermishevsky, is struck in Balakhani, flowing 90 million poods (~10.8 million barrels) of oil within three months.

Robert Nobel (the eldest Nobel brother) makes his first visit to the Absheron peninsula.

The world's first oil shipping service begins operating in the Caspian Sea. The brothers Nikolay and Dmitry Artemyevs of Astrakhan organize marine transportation of oil from Baku to Astrakhan using barges (bulk schooners).

Construction begins of the "Black City" oil refining district in Baku.

Baku engineer A.A. Tavrizov develops a continuous oil refining process.

1874

The Baku Oil Society (BOS), Russia's first vertically integrated company, is established based on the oil refinery plant in Surakhani. Among the founders of the BOS is the prominent industrialist Vasili Kokorev. The BOS is one of the first to drill a well developing the Balakhani-Sabunchi petroliferous formation.

John Franklin Carll produces subsurface contour maps of oil-bearing strata in northwestern Pennsylvania, notably the Venango Third Sand.

1875

The Nobel brothers Robert, Ludwig, and Alfred begin their work in the Azerbaijani oil business.

Industrial development of oil fields in the Baku settlements of Sabunchi, Zabrat, and Romany begins.

Oil industrialist Victor Ragozin begins industrial production of lubricating oils in Azerbaijan.

The firm of H.Z. Tagiyev becomes the first company to engage in large-scale production of gasoline in its Bayil, Baku, factory.

October 14: A powerful gusher is struck 315 feet deep in Balakhani, flowing 150,000 poods (~18,000 barrels) per day. The gusher is on a site belonging to the Souchastniki (Participators) firm.

1876

Robert Nobel manually drills his family's first well, at Sabunchi.

Ivanitsky's deep pump is first used in the Baku oil fields.

Vladimir Shukhov invents a steam-atomizing burner for oil incineration.

Charles Alexander Mentry of the California Star Oil Works Company drills Pico Canyon Well No. 4, the discovery well of the Newhall field in southern California. It is considered California's first commercial well.

1877

The world's first modern oil tanker, *Zoroaster,* steam powered and with a steel outer layer, is constructed in Motala, Sweden, for the Nobels. Designed by Ludvig Nobel and Sven Almqvist, it runs on oil residue. It will carry its first shipment in 1878.

The excise tax on production of kerosene from crude oil is abolished in the Russian Empire.

Ludvig Nobel publishes an article "Overview of Baku petroleum industry and ideas about its future," proposing a general plan for the development of the oil industry in the Russian Empire.

Dmitri Mendeleev publishes the book *The Oil Industry in the North-American State of Pennsylvania and in the Caucasus* in Saint Petersburg.

Prolific inventor Vladimir Shukhov becomes chief engineer, at the age of twenty-five, of a new Baku branch of Alexander Bari's Moscow-headquartered construction company.

Samuel Van Syckel patents a continuous distillation process that he has been working on since 1862.

1878

September 27: The first oil gusher is struck in Bibi-Eibat. Oil fields of H.Z. Tagiyev and K. Zubalov located there eventually become large enterprises.

Engineers V. Bari and V.G. Shukhov design and build the first oil pipeline in the Russian Empire. It runs 5.6 miles from Balakhani to Black City, Baku, and is three inches in diameter. The pipeline is built for the Nobel Brothers company.

The oil company and trading firm Caspian Partnership is established by L. de Boer (Debuer), S. Baghirov, and A. Madatov.

John D. Rockefeller establishes the Tank Car Trust to buy railroad tank cars for his Union Tank Line.

1879

March 24: The Baku Branch of the Imperial Russian Technical Society (BB IRTS) is established. It will play a key role in the advancement of Baku's oil industry. The first chairman of the BB IRTS is mining engineer P.P. Semyannikov, with technologist V.B. Abramovich as secretary. The branch initially has 122 members. The BB IRTS building is still intact in Baku on Nizami Street, Building 115.

The Nobel Brothers Petroleum Production Company (*Tovarishchestvo Nephtanavo Proisvodtsva Bratiev Nobel*), or "Branobel," is established in Baku, with capital assets of 3 million rubles.

A second Baku oil pipeline, this one between Balakhani and Black City, 7.5 miles long and three inches in diameter comes into service. It is constructed under the supervision of engineers V. Bari and V.G. Shukhov.

The tanker *Surakhani*, with a capacity of more than 300,000 poods (~39,200 barrels) of kerosene, is built at the Crichton Yard shipyard in Sweden for the Baku Oil Society.

Construction of the Sabunchi-Black City railway is completed, and the first electrical station is built in Balakhani.

Tidewater Pipeline Company builds the first long-distance crude oil pipeline, six inches in diameter and 109 miles long, from Coryville in the Bradford oil district to Williamsport, Pennsylvania.

1880

On May 1 a governmental decree is issued, granting foreign citizens access to oil fields in the Baku area.

Nobel brothers begin selling gasoline.

Ludvig Nobel completes the design of the tanker *Moses*, using the hull of the vessel as the wall of a bulk cargo hold.

1881

The Nobel brothers begin transporting oil and oil products in labeled railway tanks.

Standard oil begins constructing the National Transit Pipe Line System, two six-inch lines between Olean, New York, and Saddle River, New Jersey.

Dmitri Mendeleev outlines a continuous distillation process and tests it at the Konstantinovo refinery of V.I. Ragozin.

1882

John D. Rockefeller creates the Standard Oil Trust, headquartered in New York City, uniting Standard Oil (Ohio) and various affiliated companies under one umbrella, in a deliberately opaque and confusing structure.

Ludvig Nobel develops and patents a continuous distillation process based on Dmitri Mendeleev's ideas. The Nobel brothers begin applying the process to produce high-quality kerosene efficiently.

Herman Frasch develops a process for desulfurizing crude oil. He improves the process over the next decade, and it will become crucial in enabling Standard Oil to refine high-sulfur oil from the Lima-Indiana oil field.

1883

On May 16 the Rothschild brothers (Alphonse and Edmond) establish the company Caspian and Black Sea Oil Production and Trading Company in Baku. The chief engineer is David Landau—the father of the future Nobel Prize winner in physics (1962), Lev Landau.

The shell still battery for continuous distillation, designed by V.G. Shukhov and I.I. Yelin, based on Mendeleev's method, begins operations at the Nobel Brothers' Baku refinery. In the United States, Mendeleev's method is first used in 1899.

Construction of the Trans-Caucasian Railway between Baku and Batum is completed, and rail transportation of oil begins between Baku and the Black Sea.

1884

The Council of Baku Oilmen is established, initially headed by Ludvig Nobel. Dmitri Mendeleev participates in the first session.

The oil partnership S.M. Shibayev Sidor & Co is established. It will run until 1898.

Baku engineer Otto Lents designs a machine for cable-tool drilling in which the balance beam is replaced with a drum. This method is the first automatic free-falling tool to be created for the Baku oil fields. Lents is the first to include a thrust cage for turning the tool automatically.

The giant Brea field is discovered in California.

1885

Engineer G.V. Alexeev, for the first time in the world, designs and constructs a permanent industrial unit in S.M. Shibayev's Baku factory for the production of gasoline and kerosene by cracking oil tar.

May 19: Benjamin Faurot makes the first oil discovery in the Lima-Indiana field near Lima, Allen County, Ohio.

1886

The oil tanker *Svet* delivers Baku kerosene from Batum to London.

In July the oil tanker *Gluckauf* delivers its first cargo of American oil at Geestemunde in Germany.

1887

Two new oil companies, Russian Standard and Naghiyev Musa, are established in Baku.
The giant Coalinga field is discovered in California.
The Rothschilds gain control of the Mazut company and acquire a fleet of Caspian tankers and Volga barges.

1888

October 8–9: Russian emperor Alexander III (1845–1894) visits Baku with his family. He visits the Nobel Brothers factory, the Rothschild oilfields, and Shamsi Asadullayev's oilfields in Balakhani and Sabunchi.
Vladimir Shukhov develops the distillation tube, allowing finer control over the quality of petroleum products. Two years later he receives a patent for the invention. In Baku the distillation tubes are put into use at refineries of the Nobel Brothers and others.
F. Inchick and V. Shukhov receive a patent for their highly efficient continuous fractional distillation apparatus. The apparatus is installed at the Baku plants of Shibayev and the Rothschilds. The Shibayev refinery will operate for more than forty years.
Geologist Israel White applies the anticlinal theory to discover the Mannington oil field in West Virginia.

1889

The Russian Nobel Prize, named for Ludvig Nobel is established, for outstanding innovations in metallurgy or the oil industry. This is different from the more famous Nobel Prize named for Ludvig's brother Alfred. The Ludvig Nobel prize will be awarded three times, in 1896, 1898, and 1905.

1890

The US Congress passes the Sherman Antitrust Act prohibiting various activities restricting interstate commerce and market competition. The act is largely inspired by Standard Oil's business practices.
Baku engineer K.G. Simchenko develops a rotary drill. He will receive a patent five years later.
Lyman Stewart, Wallace Hardison, and Thomas R. Bard form the Union Oil Company of California.

1891

Vladimir Shukhov and Sergei Gavrilov receive a patent for continuous thermal cracking with tubular distillation. This is a revolutionary process that greatly increases gasoline yields from crude oil. It predates the US Burton process by twenty-four years. The Burton process will achieve much more commercial success, partly because the Shukhov process is developed at a time when global demand for gasoline in transportation applications has not yet matured.

1892

March 2: The Ohio Supreme Court convicts Standard Oil of violating the Sherman Antitrust Act. Despite the ruling, the Standard Oil Trust continues to operate for several years.

November: Edward Doheny and Charles Canfield discover the Los Angeles City oil field.

November 28: Albert P. McBride and Camden L. Bloom make the first commercial oil discovery in the US Mid-Continent Oil Region, with their Norman No. 1 Well near Neodesha, Kansas.

1894

The giant Midway-Sunset field is discovered in California.

June 9: The Corsicana Oil Field is discovered in Texas, heralding the beginning of the modern Texas oil industry.

1896

The first salt-water wells in the United States are drilled over the water close to the shore, to exploit an offshore extension of the Summerland oil field in Santa Barbara County, California.

1897

The oilfields of H.Z. Tagiyev are bought by English industrialists J. Vishaw, E. Hubbard, and others, who organize the Russian Oil Petroleum and Liquid Fuel Company.

Construction of the world's largest kerosene pipeline, paralleling the Trans-Caucasian Railway route between Baku and Batum, begins. The pipeline, with a total length of 547 miles, will take ten years and cost 50 million rubles to complete.

15 April: Albert P. McBride and Camden L. Bloom drill the Nellie Johnstone No. 1. Well, discovering the Bartlesville-Dewey field in Oklahoma.

1898

The Rothschild brothers (Alphonse and Edmond) establish a trading and transportation Company, Mazut, in Baku; by 1912 it will have thirteen oil tankers sailing the Caspian, plus tows and other auxiliary ships.

In summer, American oil industry engineers from Standard Oil investigate the Shemakhy district near Baku and predict industrial reserves of oil there. Later (in 1912), the famous geologist N. Lebedev will confirm these results.

The Baku Society of Russian Oil Company is established in London and immediately begins operation. By 1914 the company will have produced 5.14 million poods (~617,000 barrels) of oil.

1899

Standard Oil reorganizes as Standard Oil (New Jersey), taking advantage of favorable New Jersey laws allowing corporations to hold stock in other corporations. Assets formerly in the Standard Oil Trust are put into the Standard Oil (New Jersey) holding company.

The giant Kern River field is discovered in California.

1900

Several oil companies are established in Baku, including the Alexander Benkendorf company, with a startup capital of 4 million rubles; the English Bibi-Eibat Petroleum Co. Ltd., with a startup capital of 460,000 pounds sterling; the English Balakhani Syndicate Limited, with a startup capital of 100,000 pounds sterling; and the Absheron Oil Society, with a startup capital of 2.7 million rubles.

Mining engineer Nikolai Lebedev opens the Geological Bureau in Baku to render technical assistance to the oil industry.

Railways are completed connecting Baku with a pan-Russian market, including one between Balajari, Baku, and Petrovsk (now Mahachkala) Russia.

Selected events after 1900:

1901

January 10: Anthony Lucas discovers the Spindletop Oil Field, initiating the first Texas oil boom.

1904

August 24: A gusher heralds the beginning of major production in Surakhani.
November: A second Russian Nobel Prize, in honor of Emanuel Nobel (Ludvig Nobel's son) is established in Baku, to recognize inventions and advancements in the oil industry with an award of 1,000 rubles. It is awarded four times: in 1909, 1910, 1911, and 1914.

1911

May 15: Standard Oil is finally dissolved into thirty-four independent companies by order of the US Supreme Court.

1912

The Rothschilds sell their Azerbaijan oil interests to Royal Dutch Shell.

1914–1918

First World War. Oil, especially American oil, plays a significant role in Allied victory.

1918

June 2: Baku Council of People's Commissars issues a decree declaring the oil industry the property of the people.
June 20: Vladimir Lenin signs a decree nationalizing the oil industry in Russia.

1920

May 24: Azerbaijan Revolutionary Committee issues a decree formally nationalizing the oil industry in Azerbaijan.
November 14: The Baku Polytechnic Institute is established. It is the first institution of higher learning in Europe and Asia devoted to training scientists and engineers for all branches of the oil industry.

Appendix D

Statistical Tables

Table D.1. Officially Recorded Oil Production in the Main Producing Countries, 1857–1900 (Thousands of Barrels)

Year	*World*	*United States*	*Azerbaijan (Russian Empire)*	*Galicia (Austria-Hungary)*	*Romania*	*Canada*
1857	2				2	
1858	4				4	
1859	6	2			4	
1860	509	500			9	
1861	2,131	2,114			17	
1862	3,092	3,057			23	12
1863	2,763	2,611	41		28	83
1864	2,304	2,116	65		33	90
1865	2,716	2,498	67		39	110
1866	3,899	3,598	83		42	175
1867	3,709	3,347	120		51	190
1868	3,990	3,646	88		56	200
1869	4,696	4,215	202		59	220
1870	5,799	5,261	205		83	250
1871	5,730	5,205	165		90	270
1872	6,877	6,293	185		91	308
1873	10,838	9,894	475		104	365
1874	11,938	10,927	583	150	103	169
1875	9,977	8,788	697	159	108	220
1876	11,051	9,133	1,320	164	111	312
1877	15,754	13,350	1,801	170	108	312

(Continued)

Table D.1. (Continued)

Year	*World*	*United States*	*Azerbaijan (Russian Empire)*	*Galicia (Austria-Hungary)*	*Romania*	*Canada*
1878	18,417	15,397	2,401	176	109	312
1879	23,601	19,914	2,761	215	110	575
1880	30,018	26,286	3,001	229	115	350
1881	31,993	27,661	3,602	286	122	275
1882	35,704	30,350	4,538	330	136	275
1883	30,255	23,450	6,002	365	139	250
1884	35,969	24,218	10,805	408	211	250
1885	36,765	21,859	13,925	465	194	250
1886	47,243	28,065	18,006	305	169	584
1887	47,807	28,283	18,368	344	182	526
1888	52,165	27,612	23,049	467	219	695
1889	61,507	35,163	24,610	515	298	705
1890	76,633	45,824	28,691	659	383	795
1891	91,100	54,293	34,573	631	488	755
1892	88,739	50,515	35,775	646	593	780
1893	92,038	48,431	40,457	693	536	798
1894	89,336	49,344	36,376	949	507	829
1895	103,663	52,892	46,140	1,453	575	726
1896	114,159	60,960	47,221	2,443	543	727
1897	121,949	60,476	54,399	2,226	571	710
1898	124,925	55,364	61,609	2,376	776	758
1899	131,144	57,071	65,955	2,313	1,426	809
1900	149,132	63,621	75,779	2,347	1,629	914

Source: Stowell (1885); Oliphant (1901); Day (1922).

Where necessary, values have been converted from poods to barrels using a density of 0.859 g/cc for Azerbaijani oil (Day 1922). At that density, a barrel is equivalent to 8.3374 poods.

Table D.2. Estimates of Azerbaijani Oil Production before 1862, in Barrels

Year	*Production*	*Year*	*Production*
1818	29,026	1840	27,393
1819	29,026	1841	27,467
1820	29,026	1842	27,814
1821	23,988	1843	27,575
1822	23,988	1844	27,643
1823	23,988	1845	28,114
1824	25,289	1846	28,694
1825	29,026	1847	30,623
1826	29,986	1848	32,709
1827	29,986	1849	30,168
1828	29,986	1850	31,185
1829	29,986	1851	No data
1830	29,986	1852	No data
1831	29,986	1853	No data

Year	Production	Year	Production
1832	31,305	1854	No data
1833	21,590	1855	26,084
1834	28,241	1856	No data
1835	28,481	1857	26,387
1836	28,618	1858	No data
1837	27,649	1859	No data
1838	28,071	1860	29,723
1839	28,071	1861	No data

Source: Pazhitnov (1940).

Note: Values have been converted from poods to barrels using a density of 0.859 g/cc for Azerbaijani oil (Day 1922). At that density, a barrel is equivalent to 8.3374 poods.

Table D.3. Oil Production in Selected US States, 1859–1900, Thousands of Barrels

Year	Pennsylvania	Ohio	West Virginia	California	Indiana	Texas
1859	2					
1860	500					
1861	2,114					
1862	3,057					
1863	2,611					
1864	2,116					
1865	2,498					
1866	3,598					
1867	3,347					
1868	3,646					
1869	4,215					
1870	5,261					
1871	5,205					
1872	6,293					
1873	9,894					
1874	10,927					
1875	8,788					
1876	8,969	32	120	12		
1877	13,135	30	172	13		
1878	15,163	38	180	15		
1879	19,685	29	180	20		
1880	26,028	39	179	41		
1881	27,377	34	151	100		
1882	30,054	40	128	129		

(Continued)

Table D.3. (Continued)

Year	Pennsylvania	Ohio	West Virginia	California	Indiana	Texas
1883	23,128	48	126	143		
1884	23,772	90	90	262		
1885	20,776	662	91	325		
1886	25,798	1,783	102	377		
1887	22,356	5,023	145	679		
1888	16,489	10,011	119	690		
1889	21,487	12,471	544	303	33	0.05
1890	28,458	16,125	493	307	63	0.05
1891	33,009	17,740	2,406	324	137	0.05
1892	28,422	16,363	3,810	385	698	0.05
1893	20,315	16,250	8,445	470	2,335	0.05
1894	19,020	16,792	8,578	706	3,689	0.06
1895	19,144	19,545	8,120	1,208	4,386	0.05
1896	20,584	23,941	10,020	1,253	4,681	1.45
1897	19,262	21,561	13,090	1,903	4,122	66
1898	15,948	18,739	13,615	2,257	3,731	546
1899	14,375	21,142	13,911	2,642	3,848	669
1900	14,559	22,363	16,196	4,099	4,874	836

Source: Day (1922). Pennsylvania includes New York production.

Table D.4. Officially Recorded Oil Production in Azerbaijani Giant Fields, 1889–1900 (Thousands of Barrels)

Year	Balakhani	Sabunchi	Romani	Bibi-Eibat
1889	8,424	12,905		2,173
1890	7,743	17,525	189	2,204
1891	9,068	19,992	1,585	2,920
1892	7,026	18,917	5,017	4,066
1893	7,070	17,884	8,943	5,806
1894	7,217	17,485	7,543	4,130
1895	8,259	18,500	13,620	5,761
1896	10,470	18,664	9,546	8,540
1897	11,774	20,407	11,822	7,642
1898	12,921	22,396	12,292	11,800
1899	14,041	28,210	12,052	9,903
1900	15,242	30,762	14,039	13,400

Source: Stowell (1885); Oliphant (1901).

Notes: Balakhani, Sabunchi, and Romani are commonly considered to comprise a single giant field complex.

The Surakhani area has seen exploitation of its oil resources since ancient times. The Surakhani giant field was first discovered in a modern sense in 1870. However, it did not begin very large-scale production until the twentieth century. A gusher drilled on August 24, 1904, heralded the beginning of major production (Mir-Babayev 2008).

Values have been converted from poods to barrels using a density of 0.859 g/cc for Azerbaijani oil (Day 1922). At that density, a barrel is equivalent to 8.3374 poods.

Table D.5. Oil Production from US Giant Fields in the Nineteenth Century, Thousands of Barrels

Year	Bradford	Lima-Indiana
1871	1	
1872	2	
1873	2	
1874	3	
1875	25	
1876	383	
1877	1,468	
1878	6,209	
1879	13,915	
1880	22,212	
1881	22,945	
1882	17,959	
1883	13,295	
1884	11,883	
1885	10,564	
1886	9,753	1,138
1887	7,581	4,650
1888	5,306	9,653
1889	5,765	12,187
1890	5,609	15,078
1891	5,452	17,453
1892	4,291	15,868
1893	3,502	15,982
1894	3,360	17,297
1895	3,245	20,237
1896	3,605	25,256
1897	3,904	22,805
1898	3,444	20,321
1899	3,207	20,225
1900	3,022	21,759

Source: Fettke (1938, 292); Day (1922).

Table D.6. Oil Prices in US$ per Barrel, 1861–1900, in Money of the Day and Constant 2019 Dollars

Year	US$, Money of the Day	US$ 2019 Money
1861	0.49	13.89
1862	1.05	26.78
1863	3.15	65.14
1864	8.06	131.21
1865	6.59	109.62

(Continued)

Table D.6. (Continued)

Year	US$, Money of the Day	US$ 2019 Money
1866	3.74	65.04
1867	2.41	43.90
1868	3.63	69.44
1869	3.64	69.63
1870	3.86	77.72
1871	4.34	92.24
1872	3.64	77.36
1873	1.83	38.90
1874	1.17	26.33
1875	1.35	31.30
1876	2.56	61.21
1877	2.42	57.86
1878	1.19	31.40
1879	0.86	23.50
1880	0.95	25.07
1881	0.86	22.69
1882	0.78	20.58
1883	1.00	27.33
1884	0.84	23.80
1885	0.88	24.94
1886	0.71	20.12
1887	0.67	18.99
1888	0.88	24.94
1889	0.94	26.64
1890	0.87	24.65
1891	0.67	18.99
1892	0.56	15.87
1893	0.64	18.14
1894	0.84	24.72
1895	1.36	41.62
1896	1.18	36.11
1897	0.79	24.18
1898	0.91	27.85
1899	1.29	39.48
1900	1.19	36.42

Note: From data in BP (2020).

References

Aalto, K. R. 2013. "Petrolia, California's First Oil Field—A Century of Disappointment." *Oil-Industry History* 12, no. 1: 71–76.

Abich, H. W. von. 1864. "Étude sur les presqu'iles de Kertsch et de Taman." *Bulletin de la Société Géologique de France*. 2nd ser. 21: 259–79.

ACAC. 1884. "Acts Collected by the Caucasian Archeographic Commission." *Tbilisi* 9: 112.

———. 1885. "Acts Collected by the Caucasian Archeographic Commission." *Tbilisi* 10: 1143.

Adomites, Paul, and Ed Bernik. 2010. *Pennsylvania Crude, Boomtowns and Oil Barons*. Bradford, PA: Forest Press.

Alekperov, Vagit. 2011. *Oil of Russia*. Minneapolis, MN: East View Press.

Alizadeh, Akif A., Ibrahim S. Guliyev, Fakhraddin A. Kadirov, and Lev V. Eppelbaum. 2016. *Geosciences of Azerbaijan, Volume 1: Geology*. Cham, Switzerland: Springer International.

———. 2017. *Geosciences of Azerbaijan, Volume 2: Economic Geology and Applied Geophysics*. Cham, Switzerland: Springer International.

Andrews, E. B. 1861. "Rock Oil, its Geological Relations and Distribution." *American Journal of Science*. 2nd ser. 32: 85–93.

Ash, Mary Ellen. 2016. "The Friar and the Oil Spring." *Oil-Industry History* 17, no. 1: 59–72.

Ashburner, C. A. 1880. *Geology of McKean County*. Harrisburg, PA: Second Geological Survey of Pennsylvania, Report of Progress R.

BakIzv. 1883. Bakinskiye Izvestiya, no. 5.

Baku Branch. 1886. *Transactions of the Baku Branch of the Imperial Russian Technical Society,* No. 1. Baku, Azerbaijan.

Balayev, S. G. 1969. *Oil in the Country of Eternal Fire*. Baku: Azerneshr Publishing House.

Beaton, Kendall. 1955. "Dr. Gesner's Kerosene: The Start of American Oil Refining." *Business History Review* 29, no. 1: 28–53.

BP. 2020. *BP Statistical Review of World Energy*. 69th ed. London: BP, plc.

Brice, William R. 2002. "Abraham Gesner (1797–1864)—A Petroleum Pioneer." *Oil-Industry History* 3, no. 1: 72–80.

———. 2008. "Samuel M. Kier (1813–1874)—The Oft-Forgotten Oil Pioneer." *Oil-Industry History* 9, no. 1: 73–96.

———. 2009. *Myth, Legend, Reality: Edwin Laurentine Drake and the Early Oil Industry*. Oil City, PA: Oil Region Alliance.

———. 2010. "The Drake Well and Unintended Consequences." *Oil-Industry History* 11, no. 1: 61–83.

———. 2011. "Ebenezer Baldwin Andrews (1821–1880)—Pioneer Oil Geologist." *Oil-Industry History* 12, no. 1: 13–44.

Camp, Mark J. 2016. *On a Handshake, Humble Beginnings to Global Impact: Ohio's Oil and Gas Industry*. San Antonio, TX: HPNbooks.

Carll, John F. 1874. *Report of Progress in the Venango County District*. Harrisburg, PA: Board of Commissioners for the Second Geological Survey.

———. 1880. *The Geology of the Oil Regions of Warren, Venango, Clarion, and Butler Counties*. Harrisburg, PA: Board of Commissioners for the Second Geological Survey.

Carll, John F. 1890. *Seventh Report on the Oil and Gas Fields of Western Pennsylvania. For 1887, 1888*. Harrisburg, PA: Board of Commissioners for the Geological Survey.

Carmalt S. W., and Andrea Moscariello. 2017. "What is a Giant Field?" In *Giant fields of the Decade 2000–2010: AAPG Memoir 113*, edited by R. K. Merrill and C. A. Sternbach, 9–14. Tulsa, OK: American Association of Petroleum Geologists.

Chandler, Alfred D. 1977. *The Visible Hand: The Managerial Revolution in American Business*. Cambridge, MA: Harvard University Press.

Chernow, Ron. 1998. *Titan: The Life of John D. Rockefeller Senior*. New York: Random House.

CLOWPG. 1918. *Collection of Legalizations and Orders of the Workers' and Peasants' Government for 1918*, No. 546, 551–52. CLOWPG. St. Petersburg, Russia.

Coleman, James L. Jr. 1996. "The American Whale Oil Industry: A Look Back to the Future of the American Petroleum Industry?" *Transactions of the 1995 AAPG Mid-Continent Section Meeting*: 1–21.

Davis, Margaret L. 1998. *Dark Side of Fortune: Triumph and Scandal in the Life of Oil Tycoon Edward L. Doheny*. Berkeley: University of California Press.

Day, David T., ed. 1922. *A Handbook of the Petroleum Industry*, Vol. 1. New York: John Wiley & Sons.

DeGolyer and MacNaughton. 2018. *Twentieth Century Petroleum Statistics*. 74th ed. Houston: DeGolyer and MacNaughton.

———. 2020. *Twentieth Century Petroleum Statistics: Historical Data*. Houston: DeGolyer and MacNaughton.

Derrick. 1898. *The Derrick's Hand-Book of Petroleum: A Complete Chronological and Statistical Review of Petroleum Developments from 1859 to 1898*. Oil City, PA: Derrick Publishing Company.

De Rudder, Orlando. 1997. *Alfred Nobel (1833–1896)*. Paris: Denoël.

Devereaux, Linda E. 1995. "Barret, Lyne Taliaferro. Handbook of Texas Online." Accessed October 8, 2021. https://www.tshaonline.org/handbook/entries/barret-lyne-taliaferro.

Dickey, Parke A. 1941. *Oil Geology of the Titusville Quadrangle, Pennsylvania.* 4th Series, Bulletin M22. Harrisburg, PA: Pennsylvania Geological Survey.

Dimancescu, Dan. 2020. *Oil Stories from Where it all Started in Romania.* Concord, MA: BTF Press.

DMS. 1844. "Archives of the Imperial Russian Department for Mines and Salt." File No. 2465, Section 4, Table 2.

Douet, James. 2020. *The Heritage of the Oil Industry.* The International Committee for the Conservation of the Industrial Heritage.

Drake Well. 2021. *McClintock Well No. 1: The World's Oldest Continuously Producing Oil Well.* Titusville, PA: Drake Well Museum and Park. Accessed September 25, 2021. https://www.drakewell.org/what-to-see-and-do/mcclintock-well-1.

EIA. 2012. *Annual Energy Review 2011.* Washington, DC: Energy Information Administration, U.S. Department of Energy.

———. 2020. *Refinery Capacity Report.* Washington, DC: Energy Information Administration, U.S. Department of Energy.

Eichwald, Eduard. 1834. *Reise auf dem caspischen Meere und in den Caucasus: Unternommen in den Jahren 1825–1826.* Stuttgart: J.G. Cotta.

Emmons, S. F. 1898. "Geological Excursion through Southern Russia." *Transactions of the American Institute of Mining Engineers* XXVIII: 3–23.

Fages, Pedro. 1775. "A Historical, Political, and Natural Description of California. Translated by Herbert J. Priestley." *The Catholic Historical Review* 4, no. 4 (January 1919): 486–509.

Fettke, Charles R. 1938. *The Bradford Oil Field, Pennsylvania and New York.* 4th Series, Bulletin M21. Harrisburg, PA: Pennsylvania Geological Survey.

Flaherty, Kathy J. 2010. "In the Boots of Guffey and Galey." *Oil-Industry History* 11, no. 1: 137–52.

Folsom, John. 1995. "Oil Springs, Texas. Handbook of Texas Online." Accessed October 8, 2021. https://www.tshaonline.org/handbook/entries/oil-springs-tx.

Fooks, I. G., and V. A. Matishev. 2000. *Illustrated Stories of the History of Russian Oil and Gas Business. Part I.* Moscow: Neft-Gas Publishers.

Frank, Alison Fleig. 2005. *Oil Empire: Visions of Prosperity in Austrian Galicia.* Cambridge, MA: Harvard University Press.

Frehner, Brian. 2011. *Finding Oil: The Nature of Petroleum Geology, 1859–1920.* Lincoln, NE: University of Nebraska Press.

Gesner, Abraham. 1861. *Practical treatise on Coal, Petroleum and Other Distilled Oils.* New York: Bailliere Brothers.

Gmelin, S. G. 1771. *Reise durch Russland zur Untersuchung d. drei Naturreiche, Part 4, Years of 1770–1784.* Saint Petersburg: Panteleev Brothers.

Gorny. 1872. *Gorny Journal*, no. 3.

Gray, Earle. 2008a. *Ontario's Petroleum Legacy: The Birth, Evolution and Challenges of a Global Industry.* Edmonton, Alberta: Heritage Community Foundation.

———. 2008b. "Gesner, Williams and the Birth of the Oil Industry." *Oil-Industry History* 9, no. 1: 11–23.

Griffiths, A. E., V. R. Begliarbekov, M. A. Shakbazov, and P. Sultanov. 2001. "Increasing Production from Old, Onshore Oil Fields, Azerbaijan – a Case Study." *Petroleum Geoscience* 7: 65–73.

Grosbard, Alan. 2002. "Treadwell Wharf in the Summerland, California Oil Field: The First Sea Wells in Petroleum Exploration." *Oil Industry History* 3, no. 1: 1–18.

Gruy, H. J. 2000. History of the Ownerships of Mineral Rights. *Paper presented at the Society of Petroleum Engineers Annual Technical Conference and Exhibition, Dallas, Texas, October 2000*. Paper Number SPE-63058.

Hambly, Gavin R. G. 2007. "Iran During the Reign of Fath Ali Shah and Muhammad Shah." In *The Cambridge History of Iran, Volume 7: From Nadir Shah to the Islamic Republic*, edited by Peter Avery, Gavin Hamblin, and Charles Melville, 144–73. New York: Cambridge University Press.

Hanks, Henry G. 1884. *Fourth Annual Report of the State Mineralogist*. Sacramento, CA: California State Mining Bureau.

Harper, John A. 1998. "Drake Well Memorial Park: A Little Geology, a Little History." In *Geotectonic Environment of the Lake Erie Crustal Block, 63rd Annual Conference of Pennsylvania Geologists*, edited by John A. Harper and Gary M. Fleeger, 34–80. Harrisburg, PA: Field Conference of Pennsylvania Geologists.

———. 2001. "The Incredible John F. Carll: The World's First Petroleum Geologist and Engineer." *Oilfield Journal* (Winter 2001–2002): 2–14.

———. 2013. "History and Geology of the Giant Bradford Oil Field, McKean County, PA and Cattaraugus County, NY." *Oil-Industry History* 14, no. 1: 19–32.

Henderson, Kenneth P. 2001. "A History of Oil Production in California." *Oil Industry History* 2, no. 2: 1–8.

Henry, J. T. 1873. *The Early and Later History of Petroleum, with Authentic Facts in Regard to its Development in Western Pennsylvania*. Philadelphia, PA: Jas. B. Rodgers Co.

Hildreth, S. P. 1826. "Facts Relating to Certain Parts of the State of Ohio." *The American Journal of Science and Arts* 10: 1–8.

———. 1833. "Observations on the Saliferous Rock Formation, in the Valley of the Ohio." *The American Journal of Science and Arts* 24 (July): 46–68.

Historic Marker Database. 2022. "Burning Spring Monument." Accessed February 28, 2022. https://www.hmdb.org/m.asp?m=169958.

Hodgson, Susan Fox. 2003. "California Indians, Artisans of Oil." *Oil Industry History* 4, no. 1: 42–54.

Horn, Mike. 2021. *Giant Oil and Gas Fields of the World. Digital Dataset*. Cambridge, MA: Harvard University Center for Geographic Analysis. Accessed April 10, 2021. http://worldmap.harvard.edu/data/geonode:giant_oil_gas_fields_of_the_world_vbj.

Hunt, Thomas Sterry. 1862. "Notes on the History of Petroleum or Rock Oil." *Smithsonian Institution Annual Report* (1861): 319–29.

Hyne, Norman J. 2015. "Glenn Pool—The Start of the Oklahoma Oil Boom." *Oil-Industry History* 16, no. 1: 21–24.

Kaiser, Brooks. 2017. *The Transition from Whale Oil to Petroleum. Workshop on Past Energy Transitions: Fueling Growth and the Environmental Consequences.* Esbjerg, Denmark: University of Southern Denmark. Accessed September 5, 2021. https://www.sdu.dk/-/media/files/om_sdu/institutter/miljo/energycenter/brooks+kaiser.pdf

Klass, Alexandra B., and Danielle Meinhardt. 2015. Transporting Oil and Gas: U.S. Infrastructure Challenges. *Iowa Law Review,* Vol. 100:947, 947-1053.

Larraz, Rafael. 2021. "A Brief History of Oil Refining." *Substantia* 5, no. 2: 129–52.

Mann, Alfred N. 2009. Petroleum Pioneers of Pittsburgh. *Oil-Industry History,* v. 10, no. 1, 49-68.

Mann, Alfred N. 2011. "Petroleum Pioneers of Pittsburgh—The Origins of Gulf Oil." *Oil-Industry History* 12, no. 1: 145–54.

Marvin, Charles. 1891. *The Region of the Eternal Fire: An Account of a Journey to the Petroleum Region of the Caspian in 1883, New Edition.* London: W.H. Allen and Co.

Matveichuk, Alexander A. 2002. *Russia's First Oil Engineers*. Moscow: Interdialect. (In Russian).

———. 2004. *Intersection of Oil Parallels: Historical Essays*. Moscow: Russian Oil and Gas Institute.

Mayhew, Anne. 2008. *Narrating the Rise of Big Business in the USA: How Economists Explain Standard Oil and Wal-Mart*. New York: Routledge.

McKain, David L., and Bernard L. Allen. 1994. *Where It All Began: The Story of the People and Places Where the Oil Industry Began—West Virginia and Southeastern Ohio*. Parkersburg, WV: David L. McKain.

Merriam, Daniel F. 2002. "Exploring for Petroleum in the Flatlands: History of Oil and Gas Exploration in Kansas." *Oil Industry History* 3, no. 1: 56–71.

Meyer, Warren. 2010. "The Man Who Saved the Whales." *Forbes Sites*. Accessed October 22, 2021. https://www.forbes.com/sites/warrenmeyer/2010/11/05/the-man-who-saved-the-whales/?sh=169ff87a596f.

Miesner, Thomas O., and William L. Leffler. 2006. *Oil and Gas Pipelines in Nontechnical Language*. Tulsa, OK: Pennwell.

Milanovsky, E. E. 2007. "Hermann Abich (1806–1886): 'The Father of Caucasian Geology' and His Travels in the Caucasus and Armenian Highlands." In *Four Centuries of Geological Travel: The Search for Knowledge on Foot, Bicycle, Sledge and Camel, Special Publication 287*, edited by Patrick N. Wyse Jackson, 177–81. London: The Geological Society.

Mir-Babayev, Mir-Yusif. 2008. *Concise History of Azerbaijani Oil*. Baku, Azerbaijan: Socar.

———. 2011. "The Role of Azerbaijan in the World's Oil Industry." *Oil-Industry History* 12, no. 1: 109–23.

———. 2012. "The Rothschild Brothers' Contribution to Baku's Oil Industry." *Oil-Industry History* 13, no. 1: 225–36.

———. 2013. "The Unknown Nobel Prize in Baku." *Oil-Industry History* 14, no. 1: 117–24.

———. 2015. "Baku-Batum—The World's Longest Pipeline." *Visions of Azerbaijan*, January–February 2015. Accessed October 5, 2021. http://www.visions.az/en/news/618/3b2f9122/.

———. 2017. "Brief History of the First Drilled Oil Well; and the People Involved." *Oil-Industry History* 18, no. 1: 25–34.

———. 2021. "The Bibi-Heybat Oil Field: The 175th Anniversary of the First Oil Well in the World." *AAPG Explorer* 42, no. 8: 17–21.

Montague, Gilbert Holland. 1902. The Rise and Supremacy of the Standard Oil Company. *The Quarterly Journal of Economics,* Vol. 16, No. 2, pp. 265-292.

Moser, Nat. 2018. *Oil and the Economy of Russia from the Late Tsarist to the Post-Soviet Period.* New York: Routledge.

Nordhaus, William D. 1997. "Do Real-Output and Real-Wage Measures Capture Reality? The History of Lighting Suggests Not." In *The Economics of New Goods*, edited by Timothy F. Bresnahan and Robert J. Gordon, 29–70. Chicago: University of Chicago Press.

Nuttall, Brandon C. 2014. "Of Kentucky, Salt, and Oil: A History of Early Petroleum Finds along the Cumberland River." *Oil-Industry History* 15, no. 1: 67–80.

Olien, Roger M. 1995. "Oil and Gas Industry. Handbook of Texas Online." Accessed October 8, 2021. https://www.tshaonline.org/handbook/entries/oil-and-gas-industry.

Oliphant, F. H. 1898. "Petroleum." In *Mineral Resources of the United States, 1897, Part VI (continued), Nonmetallic Products, Except Coal and Coke, Nineteenth Annual Report of the United States Geological Survey to the Secretary of the Interior 1897–1898*, edited by Charles D. Wolcott, 1–166. Washington, DC: United States Geological Survey.

———. 1901. "Petroleum." In *Mineral Resources of the United States, 1899, Part VI (continued), Nonmetallic Products, Except Coal and Coke, Twenty-First Annual Report of the United States Geological Survey to the Secretary of the Interior 1899–1900*, edited by Charles D. Wolcott, 1–294. Washington, DC: United States Geological Survey.

Owen, Edgar Wesley. 1975. *Trek of the Oil Finders: A History of Exploration for Petroleum*. Tulsa, OK: American Association of Petroleum Geologists, Memoir 6.

Pazhitnov, K. A. 1940. *Essays on the History of the Baku Oil Production Industry*. Moscow: Moscow-Leningrad.

Pees, Samuel T. 2002. "Petroleum Mining in NW Pennsylvania." *Oil-Industry History* 3, no. 1: 34–55.

Prutzman, Paul W. 1913. *Petroleum in Southern California*. Bulletin 63. Sacramento, CA: California State Mining Bureau.

RGRI. 2021. *Early Period of GeolCom (1882–1917) (Organization of a Systematic Geological Study of the Country)*. St. Petersburg: Russian Geological Research Institute. Accessed May 2021. https://vsegei.ru/en/about/history/1882-1917.php.

Rizea, Marian. 2017. "160 de ani de Industrie Petrolieră Românească (1)." *Revista ART-EMIS Academy*, May 3. Accessed May 2021. https://www.art-emis.ro/eveniment/160-de-ani-de-industrie-petroliera-romaneasca-1.

Rovinaru, Flavius-Ioan, Ioana-Sorina Mihut, and Marcel Pirvu. 2015. "The Role of the Economic Governance in the Context of the National Oil Industry. Case Study: Romana-The Beginnings (19th and 20th Century)." *Revista Economica* 67, no. 4: 131–51.

Russell, Loris S. 1968. *A Heritage of Light: Lamps and Lighting in the Early Canadian Home*. Toronto: University of Toronto Press.

Scherer, F. M. 2011. "Standard Oil as a Technological Innovator." *Review of Industrial Organization* 38, no. 3: 225–33.

SHA-Azerbaijan-a. Undated. State Historical Archives of the Republic of Azerbaijan. f.24, op.24, doc.109.

———-b. Undated. State Historical Archives of the Republic of Azerbaijan, f.24, op.24, doc. 390.

Sherrill, R. E., P. A. Dickey, and L. S. Matteson. 1941. "Types of Stratigraphic Oil Pools in Venango Sands of Northwestern Pennsylvania." In *Stratigraphic Type Oil Fields*, edited by A. I. Levorsen, N. Wood Bass, Ross L. Heaton, W. S. W. Kew, D. Perry Olcott, and Theron Wasson, 507–38. Tulsa, OK: American Association of Petroleum Geologists.

Silliman, Benjamin. 1855. *Report on the Rock Oil, or Petroleum, from Venango Co., Pennsylvania, with Special Reference to its use for Illumination and Other Purposes*. New Haven, CT: J.H. Benham.

———. 1864. *A Description of the Recently Discovered Petroleum Region of California*. New York: Francis and Loutrel.

———. 1865. *Professor Silliman's Report upon the Property of the Philadelphia and California Petroleum Company of Philadelphia Situated in Santa Barbara and Los Angeles Counties, California*. Philadelphia: E.C. Markley and Son.

Skelton, Lawrence H. 2006. "A Brief History of the Oklahoma Oil and Gas Industry." *Oil-Industry History* 7, no. 1: 79–82.

Smaje, Chris. 2020. "Why Oil Didn't Save the Whales—and Why it Matters." *Resilience.org*. Accessed October 22, 2021. https://www.resilience.org/stories/2020-06-29/why-oil-didnt-save-the-whales-and-why-it-matters/.

Smith, Julia Cauble. 1952. "Corsicana Oilfield. Handbook of Texas Online." Accessed September 15, 2021. https://www.tshaonline.org/handbook/entries/corsicana-oilfield.

Sorenson, Raymond P. 2009. "The First Reports of Oil in Oklahoma." *Oil-Industry History* 10, no. 1: 83–95.

———. 2014. "19th Century Russian Petroleum from Baku: The American Perspective." *Oil-Industry History* 15, no. 1: 91–112.

———. 2016. "Thomas Sterry Hunt's Petroleum Research (1826–1892)." *Oil-Industry History* 16, no. 1: 69–82.

———. 2020. "Pre-Drake Oil and Gas Wells." *Oil-Industry History* 21, no. 1: 79–96.

Sorkhabi, Rasoul. 2005. "Pre-Modern History of Bitumen, Oil and Gas in Persia (Iran)." *Oil-Industry History* 6, no. 1: 153–77.

Sozanski, Jozef, Stanislaw Kuk, Czeslaw Jaracz, and Piotr S. Dziadzkio. 2006. "How the Modern Oil and Gas Industry Was Born: Historical Remarks." In *The Carpathians and Their Foreland: Geology and Hydrocarbon Resources, AAPG Memoir*

84, edited by J. Golonka and F. J. Picha, 811–34. Tulsa, OK: American Association of Petroleum Geologists.

Speight, James G. 2017. *Handbook of Petroleum Refining*. Boca Raton, FL: CRC Press.

Spencer, Jeff A. 2008. "A Journey Through Two Early Ohio Oil Booms: The Northwest Ohio and the Bremen-New Straitsville Booms." *Oil-Industry History* 9, no. 1: 59–72.

Starbuck, Alexander. 1878. *History of the American Whale Fishery from its Earliest Inception to the Year 1876*. Waltham, MA: Alexander Starbuck.

Stowell, S. H. 1885. "Petroleum." In *Mineral Resources of the United States, Calendar Years 1883 and 1884*, edited by Albert Williams, Jr., 214–32. Washington, DC: United States Geological Survey.

Tarbell, Ida. 1905. *The History of the Standard Oil Company*. New York: McClure, Phillips & Co.

Testa, Stephen M. 2001. "Geologic Perceptions Regarding Oil Prospects and Future Growth and Development of California in the Post-Gold Rush Era." *Oil-Industry History* 2, no. 1: 71–86.

———. 2005. "The Los Angeles City Oil Field: California's First Oil Boom During the Revitalization Period." *Oil-Industry History* 6, no. 1: 79–100.

Thompson, A. Beeby. 1904. *The Oil Fields of Russia and the Russian Petroleum Industry*. London: Crosby Lockwood and Son.

———. 1908. *The Oil Fields of Russia and the Russian Petroleum Industry*. 2nd ed. London: Crosby Lockwood and Son.

Tiratsoo, E. N. 1984. *Oilfields of the World*. 3rd ed. Houston, TX: Gulf Publishing Company.

Tolf, Robert W. 1976. *The Russian Rockefellers*. Stanford, CA: Hoover Institution Press.

USDI. 1957. *National Survey of Historic Sites and Buildings: Pico Canyon, Well No. "CSO" 4 (Pico #4)*. Washington, DC: United States Department of the Interior, National Park Service.

Vassiliou, Marius. 2018. *Historical Dictionary of the Petroleum Industry*. 2nd ed. Lanham, MD: Rowman and Littlefield.

Waples, David A. 2005a. "Energy's Stepchild: The Birth and Rearing of the Appalachian Natural Gas Industry 1800–1950." *Oil-Industry History* 6, no. 1: 55–71.

———. 2005b. *Natural Gas Industry in Appalachia: A History from the First Discovery to the Maturity of the Industry*. Jefferson, NC: McFarland.

Webster, Ian. 2021. "Inflation Calculator." *U.S. Official Inflation Data, Alioth Finance*, September 1, 2021. Accessed September 5, 2021. https://www.officialdata.org/.

Wells, B. A., and K. L.Wells. 2021a. *First Kansas Oil Well*. Washington, DC: American Oil & Gas Historical Society. Accessed February 28, 2022. https://aoghs.org/petroleum-pioneers/kansas-mid-continent-oil-fields.

———. 2021b. *Shooters – A "Fracking" History*. Washington, DC: American Oil and Gas Historical Society. Accessed February 28, 2022. https://aoghs.org/technology/hydraulic-fracturing/.

Welty, Earl M., and Frank J. Taylor. 1966. *The 76 Bonanza: The Fabulous Life and Times of the Union Oil Company of California*. Menlo Park, CA: Lane.

Westwood, J. N. 1966. "The Vladikavkaz Railway: A Case of Enterprising Private Enterprise." *Slavic Review* 25, no. 4: 669–75.

Wheelock, T. B. 1834. Journal of Colonel Dodge's expedition from Fort Gibson to the Pawnee Pict village: *American State Papers, Military Affairs,* v. V (5), p. 373–382. Originally published as *Senate Executive Document 1,* v. 1, 23rd Congress, 2nd Session, p. 73-93.

White, I. C. 1892. "The Mannington Oil Field and the History of its Development." *Bulletin of the Geological Society of America* 3: 187–216.

White, John H., Jr. 1993. *The American Railroad Freight Car*. Baltimore: Johns Hopkins University Press.

Williamson, Harold F., and Arnold R. Daum. 1959. *The American Petroleum Industry: The Age of Illumination, 1859–1899*. Evanston, IL: Northwestern University Press.

———. 1963. *The American Petroleum Industry: The Age of Energy, 1899–1959.* Evanston, IL: Northwestern University Press.

Williams, John Alexander. 2021. "Formation of West Virginia." *e-WV: The West Virginia Encyclopedia.* 02 September 2021. Accessed August 24, 2022. https://www.wvencyclopedia.org/articles/2034.

Wrigley, Henry E. 1874. *Special report on the petroleum of Pennsylvania, its production, transportation, manufacture and statistics*. Harrisburg, PA: Board of Commissioners for the Second Geological Survey.

Wooster, Robert, and Christine Moor Sanders. 1976. "Spindletop Oilfield. Handbook of Texas Online." Accessed September 15, 2021. https://www.tshaonline.org/handbook/entries/spindletop-oilfield.

WVGES. 2004. *History of WV Mineral Industries—Oil and Gas*. West Virginia Geological and Economic Survey. Accessed September 29, 2021. http://www.wvgs.wvnet.edu/www/geology/geoldvog.htm.

Yergin, Daniel. 1991. *The Prize: The Epic Quest for Oil, Money, and Power*. New York: Simon and Schuster.

Index

Note: Page references for figures are italicized.

About the Authors

Marius Vassiliou

Marius Vassiliou is an analyst, author, adviser to government agencies, and former industrial research executive. He received a PhD in geophysics from the California Institute of Technology; an MBA from the University of California, Los Angeles; an MS in computer science from the University of Southern California; and an AB (highest honors) from Harvard University. He is the author of the *Historical Dictionary of the Petroleum Industry*, published by Rowman and Littlefield in 2009, and again in 2018 as a fully revised second edition. The second edition was selected as an Outstanding Academic Title for 2019 by the Association of College and Research Libraries (ACRL). Dr. Vassiliou was a senior research geophysicist at ARCO Oil and Gas Company and later worked on oil-industry and other problems at the Rockwell International Science Center, where he eventually rose to the position of executive director. He has had a lifelong interest in the history of petroleum. Since 2003 he has been an analyst at the Institute for Defense Analyses, where he has worked on a number of issues, including oil depletion and its implications. Dr. Vassiliou is well known for his contributions to the fields of geophysics, computational physics, and information sciences. He wrote the *Computer Professional's Quick Reference* (with J. Orenstein) and edited the *Computer Science Handbook for Displays* (with T. Huang). His book *C2 Re-envisioned: The Future of the Enterprise* (with D. S. Alberts and J. R. Agre) has been translated into Chinese. He is an active member of the Society of Exploration Geophysicists, a senior member of the Institute of Electrical and Electronics Engineers, a fellow of the Geological Society, and a licensed professional geophysicist in the state of California.

Mir-Yusif Mir-Babayev

Mir-Yusif Mir-Babayev Fazil oglu, Doctor of Chemical Sciences, is a professor at Azerbaijan Technical University, Baku, in the Department of Chemical Technology, Recycling and Ecology. Dr. Mir-Babayev is a leading specialist in the fields of oil chemistry, industrial ecology, and oil history. He was born in Baku and graduated in 1975 from the chemistry and technology faculty of the Azerbaijan Meshadi Azizbekov Petroleum and Chemistry Institute (renamed Azerbaijan State University of Oil and Industry in 2015). In 1986, he defended his thesis in "Petrochemistry" and in 1994 defended his doctoral dissertation in the same specialty. He has published more than 210 scientific works in the Azerbaijan Republic and abroad (Russia, Kazakhstan, Turkey, the United States, Great Britain, Italy, Sweden, Romania, Venezuela, Germany, and Canada). Currently, he is an oil history expert for the Baku Oil Museum, located behind the Bibi-Eibat Mosque. He is also a member of the editorial board of the journal *Azerbaijan Oil Industry* (*Azerbaijanskoe Neftyanoe Khozyaistvo*). On September 18, 2015, he was awarded the "Tərəqqi" (Progress) Medal for his achievements in the development of the Azerbaijani oil and gas industry, by decree of the president of the Azerbaijan Republic Ilham Aliyev. On September 18, 2019, he was awarded the "Fəhri Neftçi" (Honorary Oilman) medal by SOCAR, the State Oil Company of the Azerbaijan Republic.

www.ingramcontent.com/pod-product-compliance
Ingram Content Group UK Ltd.
Pitfield, Milton Keynes, MK11 3LW, UK
UKHW020841290926
15470UKWH00004B/1489

9 781793 629524